MIXING
QUILT ELEMENTS

Kathy Doughty of Material Obsession

a modern look at
COLOR, STYLE & DESIGN

stashBOOKS®
an imprint of C&T Publishing

Text copyright © 2016 by Kathy Doughty

Photography and artwork copyright © 2016 by C&T Publishing, Inc.

PUBLISHER: Amy Marson

CREATIVE DIRECTOR: Gailen Runge

EDITOR: Karla Menaugh

TECHNICAL EDITORS: Susan Nelsen and Alison M. Schmidt

COVER DESIGNER: April Mostek

BOOK DESIGNER: Christina Jarumay Fox

PRODUCTION COORDINATOR: Freesia Pearson Blizard

PRODUCTION EDITOR: Alice Mace Nakanishi

ILLUSTRATOR: Tim Manibusan

PHOTO ASSISTANT: Sarah Frost

STYLE AND FLAT PHOTOGRAPHY by John Doughty, unless otherwise noted;

INSTRUCTIONAL PHOTOGRAPHY by Diane Pedersen and Nissa Brehmer of C&T Publishing, Inc., unless otherwise noted

Published by Stash Books, an imprint of C&T Publishing, Inc.,
PO Box 1456, Lafayette, CA 94549

Library of Congress Cataloging-in-Publication Data

Doughty, Kathy, author.

 Mixing quilt elements : a modern look at color, style & design / Kathy Doughty of Material Obsession ; editor, Karla Menaugh ; illustrator, Tim Manibusan.

     pages cm

 Includes bibliographical references.

 ISBN 978-1-61745-205-5 (soft cover)

1. Quilting--Patterns. 2. Patchwork--Patterns. 3. Appliqué--Patterns. 4. Quilts--Themes, motives. I. Menaugh, Karla, 1954- editor. II. Manibusan, Tim, illustrator. III. Material Obsession (Firm) IV. Title.

 TT835.D69325 2016

 746.46--dc23

                    2015034522

Printed in China

10 9 8 7 6 5 4 3 2 1

CONTENTS

36

ACKNOWLEDGMENTS   4

PREFACE   5

INTRODUCTION   12

SEW STUDIO   14

Projects

GO SLOWLY!   25
New Star   26
Love Birds   36
Hope Hammock   44
Baby Octagon   50

WEDGE WORK   57
The Challenge   58
Wedge Log Cabin   66
Ring Around   72
Wild Child   80

AT THE MACHINE   89
Into the Woods   90
Color Works   100
Ballroom Dancing   106

MIXING TEXTURES   113
Party Favors   114
Magpie Pillows   120

ABOUT THE AUTHOR   126

RESOURCES   127

ACKNOWLEDGMENTS

Owning and operating a patchwork shop means there is always a lot to be done. My thanks go to the women of Material Obsession. I love them for their creativity, for their endless support, and for letting me be obsessive without worry. I would like to thank my Material Obsession design team: Cath Babidge, Carolyn Davis, Megan Manwaring, and Wendy Williams. These women listen to me cabbage on relentlessly about everything quilting and worldly. Without them I am nothing.

I would also like to thank the rest of the team: Bundle Caldwell, Liesel Moult, Kate Page, Robyn Shipton, and Grace Widders for their tireless efforts in the shop. Helena Fooij, our newest member, is also to be thanked for helping me with samples and patterns for this book!

Several of the quilts in this book have been quilted by others including Bhijan Attwell on Love Birds, Jan Foster on New Star, and Denise Biviano on Ballroom Dancing and Wedge Log Cabin.

And really, what kind of acknowledgment would there be without a mention for John. He drives me to be my best, never (well, hardly ever) grows weary of my energy, and reminds me of what love means in life every day. I am forever grateful for him making me better than I am. I thank my three beautiful sons for being themselves and living their creative lives with good spirit, and the rest of my family for making life interesting.

We are lucky to be quilters. I thank all of you who follow me on my blog, on Instagram, and in my books. If you buy my fabric, I love you for that. It is a beautiful community that makes life lovely to look at.

PREFACE

Every day offers us something new. If we keep our eyes and minds open, this mix creates experiences from which we can create. The blend of what we know with what we see and what we dream makes each one of us an individual. It gives us our voice. Having just recently returned from shooting the photos for this book, I am full of ideas that come from the lines of the earth. I was fascinated by the scenery that changed in a glance and overwhelmed by the harmony of mixed elements that reflected my book concept—reality and concept collided!

When John and I head out on the road to shoot the photos for these books, something amazing always happens. I have in my head what I want to do cluttered with the complications of travel. Stacks of quilts and working with the unpredictable elements of nature (not to mention my husband) can be problematic as there are so many details to consider. John has a way of always pushing me beyond where I am comfortable living. We drive long distances to reach his ideal location. We stay longer than I can stand until he has achieved the result he wants. We hurry to be in the right place to get the right light. We climb fences and rocks, jump over gullies and creeks, and generally end up in the most unbelievable locations. In the end, I am forever grateful to have ended up with a man that makes me so much better than I would have been on my own.

This trip we traveled as if the road was our own, hardly passing another car. Once out of the hustle of the city, the road wound with the curve of the seaside. I happily spotted seals basking on rocks and swimming upside down while feeding in the sea with dolphins. One look away and the earth turned crashing waves to waving, sunburned grassy paddocks. The road climbed to mountain-tops that quickly turned to steep descents down winding roads with treetops on one side and tree trunks on the other! We covered all terrain. Once we saw an echidna scurrying alongside the highway in a hurry to get somewhere safe. In an alpine location I spotted an emu that, startled by the sudden appearance of our car, dashed into the bush so fast I wondered if I had seen it all.

We stopped where we stopped. We got out, handled the quilts with care, and did our thing. It was exciting to capture the spirit of a colorful quilt flapping in the breeze against the bluest of beach skies. My hands clapped when we found a perfect deserted homestead as a backdrop for a softly colored traditional quilt. Chain-link fences accented the geometry of octagon pieces. An imaginary forest in a quilt sits among the reality of trees as if it has been there forever. The modern and the traditional concepts sat side by side, as if there is no difference at all. It's all there to see if we look.

Trees burned in long-ago fires held gray fingers to the blue sky as the bush tried to rejuvenate near their dead trunks. In a field, longing for just the right ray of sun to shine, were everlasting daisies just waiting to be picked. The dryness of the climate sucks the color out of what should be green. What is left is a washed-away sign of life that draws the eye in for a closer look at subtle beauty. Days turned to night as we aimed for an unknown hotel. In the dark we dodged countless rabbits and kangaroos of all sizes—first stunned by the dazzle of our headlights and then dashing in any direction!

10   Mixing Quilt Elements

I love the Australian landscape more every time we head out to shoot. I am grateful to be able to see so much of the land and see what the landscape has to offer to my quilts. Textiles feel weirdly at home to me when they are outside on the earth. I love that so much of this land is old, saved as it once was, and I love that my contemporary style stands proud in front of the tests of time. As I leaf through the seemingly endless pages of possible photos, I want to share them all and tell all the stories of the spaces— how the wind takes my breath, the sun warms my skin, the sinking sun makes me shiver. I hope you feel the spirit of the quilts and the land when you leaf through the pages of this book. And when you do, I hope you feel inspired to take action and make your own story of mixed elements of land, imagination, and textile. I wish a creative textile adventure for all.

So in this book I present to you a collection of quilts that features a variety of combinations. Each quilt mixes elements of design and technique while forging a new path. It is a collection of stories from the last two years. Every once in a while in the making of these quilts I found myself in unfamiliar territory. These were the times I turned to my friends for help about how to achieve what I wanted—or more likely, in a manic urge to get over the hump, I made up my own way. The point I am trying to make here is that quilting is a lifetime activity that continues to offer us achievable goals as we grow in a sharing experience. There is no reason to hold back here. Try, try, and try until you achieve a result that makes you happy. Enjoy!

INTRODUCTION

As my dad always says, "If you don't know where you are going, any road will get you there." In retrospect, I think I have lived by this motto all my life, with each step unknowingly taking me somewhere unexpected. Not knowing what I don't know never stops me from trying something new. One day so many years ago I was planning fashion shows and skateboard demos in New York City without so much as a needle in my flat … then poof, I woke up to be a quilter—

For more than two decades now I have been making quilts. It is no secret that I came to quilting later in life, but once I discovered the mystery of the quarter-inch seam, I was off and running. The desire to learn and grow my skills is seemingly endless. My fascination for squares lasted about eight years before I discovered triangles, and then that obsession took over. Straight seams and easy joins gave way to curves and inset seams. Appliqué, a skill I thought reserved for those who grew up sewing with their mothers or grandmothers, was soon a happy pastime.

Now, many years later, I have accumulated enough skills in appliqué and English paper piecing, foundation and wonky piecing, hand and machine quilting that I can do anything I want and choose the method of my madness based on my mood. There is great satisfaction in finding something new, learning it, and having a try. Mixing a variety of design methods and techniques creates new paths to unique projects. Discovering the unexpected is a thrill! The same thing can be done in lots of different ways! I used to look at a project and see what I couldn't do, but now I look for new things to learn.

The creative process can appear a mystery. I often hear people say, "I am not creative!" They say it with assurance, confirming the fact just because they say it is so. If that is you, banish the thought! Accept that everyone has creativity that comes with the freedom of confidence. Know it and make it true! Slowly, through experience, I have found this to be true myself. The urge was always there but I kept it inside. It feels better set free. The way we mix the elements of design, be it traditional, modern, or contemporary, creates a new path for expression.

Since the beginning of my quilting life I have rushed into a pile of fabric, made cuts, sewn the bits together, and loved watching the fabric cover my design wall. However, I see a new pattern developing now that involves the cross-pollination of all my skills into a hybrid style that mixes and matches all the different techniques I have acquired. In this modern era, our lives change so quickly that we hardly have time to take into account all we have learned and how it changes us before we are looking back. Somewhere along the way I have become a quilter that likes to go slow, to savor the process. Handwork appeals to me as a way to sit quietly and listen to my thoughts. Countless times I have remembered that young woman who was me, so busy doing things, always on the go. I wish she had discovered the magic of quilting to bring all the imagery of life home in her head.

So … four books later, as I planned a fifth one, I wondered what I had left to say, and this is it! Mix it up; create your own style using a variety of techniques. As always, I encourage you to have a look at the quilts here and to make them as you see them or to play with the elements in a new way. Don't let anything stop you!

SEW STUDIO

As I am making quilts for this book, I am taking into account what tools and techniques I use to make my projects easier. *Always* read through instructions to familiarize yourself with the methods used and adjust for your method if necessary. See Resources (page 127).

USEFUL TOOLS

Straight Rulers

I have standard 6½″ × 24½″ and 6½″ × 12½″ rulers on hand. I use a two-ruler method to establish the straight edge and then measure from the right to the left. Once the measurement is established, I can cut, repeat the measure, and cut again without moving the fabric. See Favorite Techniques (page 17).

Templates

Recently I have been teaching a lot of regional and international workshops, which has been a very informative experience. I have noticed that the participants who use template plastic or handmade templates instead of the readily available acrylic template rulers have more problems with accuracy. It is always good advice to check any printed templates before cutting your fabrics. I understand that purchasing a ruler is an added expense, but consider, if you will, that in most cases we have a large investment in our fabrics. A standardized ruler will provide many reliable options for using fabric with pleasing results. Commercial rulers are very accurate, can be used over and over without changing, and are very easy to use. As a self-taught quilter, I have relied on the variety of shapes and sizes to cut accurately and therefore sew more accurately when designing quilts. Ask your local shop owner to talk you through the options available, or go to the Internet where you will find so many great instructive videos.

45°/90° triangle rulers

These triangles offer an endless supply of creative options. A half-square / quarter-square triangle ruler makes short order of the math required for cutting single or double bias-edge triangles. A blunt tip on one or two points of the ruler means you can adjust the instructions to cut to the same size strip as for a square. This is handy, as often you can cut everything from one size of strip and adjust all patterns as required. It also makes sewing a bit easier because it is easy to see where to match up the pieces.

60° ruler

Six-point diamond stars, triangles, and half-triangles both vertical and horizontal are interesting shapes easily accomplished with a 60° ruler. A very handy shape that also accommodates hexagons is the Hex N More ruler by Julie Herman.

Square rulers

Trimming blocks, sizing for appliqué, centering motifs—all are easily done with large, square rulers. I have a 20½″ square and a 16½″ square, which is easier to handle for smaller blocks.

Wedge rulers

These handy rulers are a zip line to fun. They are available in a variety of degrees ranging from 10° to 22½°. Make a note of how many wedges it takes to make a circle by calculating how many times the degree goes into the full circle, 360°. For example, an 18° wedge needs 20 wedges to equal 360°.

fast2cut HexEssentials Viewers (by C&T Publishing)

These acrylic templates allow you to view the fabric design for fussy cutting and to cut hexagons with a rotary cutter. The set of small viewers includes ½″, ⅝″, ¾″, and 1″ templates. Sets for larger hexagons include 1½″ and 2½″ templates for matching hexagon, diamond, and triangle shapes.

Material Obsession 1″ Octagon and Square Set

This set includes acrylic viewers/cutting templates for octagons and squares with 1″ sides, plus packs of coordinating papers for English paper piecing.

Appliqué Tools

For techniques, see Appliqué (page 22). Handy tools include the following:

- **Needles**

  I suggest using a needle that suits you; milliners needles, sizes 9–11, work very well for appliqué. The size 11 needles are very fine and the size 9 needles are a bit sturdier.

- **Freezer paper**

  I cut pattern templates from freezer paper and iron them onto the front of the fabric.

- **Bohin chalk pencil**

  I use a chalk pencil to trace the appliqué shape onto the fabric.

- **Fabric glue stick and liquid glue**

  I use the fabric glue stick for glue-basting seam allowances on English paper piecing and use liquid glue with an applicator for double thickness appliqué such as bias stems.

- **Superior Threads Frosted Donuts**

  These sets provide a wide variety of thread colors on small spools for easy access to any color needed.

- **Circle sets**

  When the urge to make a quilt hits me, I want my tools on hand. A comprehensive set of acrylic circles or a template that cuts large circles is always a bonus. For appliqué, Perfect Circles are very handy. These are made of Mylar, so you can gather fabric around the edges and press to make a nice, crisp circle ready to be sewn onto the background. See Preparing Appliqué Circles (page 22).

- **Mary Ellen's Best Press spray starch alternative**

  This is my go-to product anytime spray starch will be used.

Design Wall

It is very important when designing quilts to use a design wall. I have a low-loft polyester batting wall in my studio for this purpose. I can cut shapes and put them on the wall to assess my progress. Checking for pattern, balance, and size is easily done on the wall. It is also possible to use a gray flannel, which is the best optical option. However, when using flannel, I generally give it a hit with basting spray to make it just a bit stickier.

Sewing Machine

I sew on a BERNINA 720. I like the fact that it has a 10″ throat. That extra width is a huge bonus if I want to do some machine quilting, and it makes quilting so much more achievable. As I familiarize myself with this machine and all the accessories, I expand my abilities! A good machine in good working order, cleaned regularly, and with a few bonus feet means you can move ahead trying new things with little trouble.

Graph Paper

Drafting a block is often a good way to remember where you have come from. I use ¼″ grid paper. The blocks are drawn up at the finished size and seam allowance is added for cutting measurements.

Thread

I use Aurifil 40-weight thread in my machine and 50-weight thread for hand sewing, generally in a soft green, gray, or beige. Lots of quality threads are available on the market.

Batting

A variety of battings can be found on the market. Assess your project, how it will be used, and how you want it to look. Hand quilting is best done using batting *without* scrim. Machine quilting is best using batting *with* scrim. Cotton and wool are best for quilts to be used in beds. I use polyester only when making wallhangings or throws. I generally use low-loft batting, which gives me a nice, flat finished quilt.

FAVORITE TECHNIQUES

Cutting Strips with Two Rulers

This method allows for easy, fast, accurate cutting of strips and saves the mat over time! When you don't use the lines on the mat to measure, you don't end up cutting in the same place all the time.

1. To start, establish a straight edge. Fold the fabric with selvages together. With the fold nearest you, position the ruler to align with the measuring lines. Trim the right-hand raw edge to be straight.

2. Position the measuring ruler along the trimmed edge, covering the strip width you wish to cut.

3. Align a second long ruler to the left of the measuring ruler.

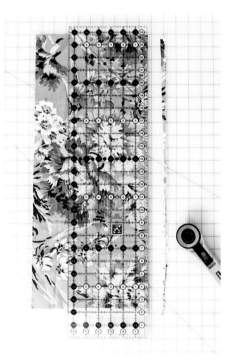

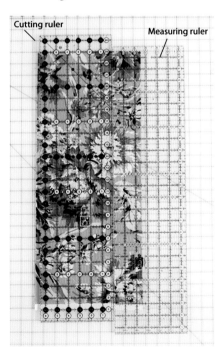

4. Remove the measuring ruler and cut against the right-hand edge of the second ruler.

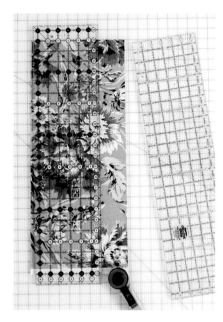

5. Repeat as many times as you like, until you have enough strips.

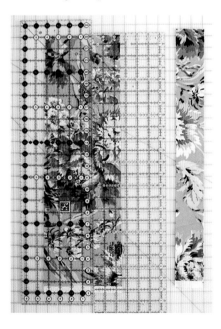

Cutting Wedges

1. Place the wedge ruler on a width-of-fabric strip. Align a straight ruler with the left edge of the template.

> **note**
>
> *Always start with the small end of the ruler at the top or the bottom of the strip when you are not using the full length of the ruler.*

2. Cut along the right edge of the wedge template.

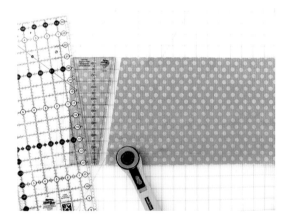

3. Remove the wedge template and cut along the right side of the straight ruler to yield the first wedge.

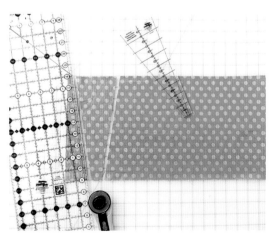

4. Rotate the wedge template and align it against the first cut. Cut along the right side to yield the second wedge.

5. Continue across the strip, alternating the template placement from top to bottom.

Wedges are so much fun to work with. If you align the narrow ends together, you will create an arc or circle. If you align the wedges head-to-tail, you will create a straight, pieced strip that can be used in sashings, borders, and more.

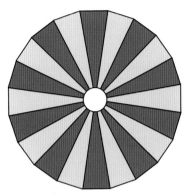

Arc or circle

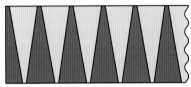

Straight strip for sashing or border

Cutting Triangles from a Strip

Follow the directions in Cutting Wedges (previous page), but substitute a 60° or 90° (quarter-square) triangle template. Use a straight ruler in tandem with the triangle template, and rotate the direction of the template as you work across the strip. No waste!

English Paper Piecing

English paper piecing is a great skill to have in your toolbox. Working fabric over papers is one of the oldest forms of traditional patchwork. It is accurate and engaging in the way fabric designs can be manipulated into new designs. Two things have made English paper piecing more popular in recent years. First is the availability of precut papers. They are accurately laser cut and available in quantities by size and shape. I use papers made by Patchwork with Busy Fingers, but there are other brands as well. The papers are cut and measured by the length of the side. For example, 1″ hexagons have six 1″ sides. The second great innovation is the fabric glue stick. Using a fabric glue stick to temporarily adhere the fabric to the papers both quickens the basting step and also makes removing the papers at the end of the process easier.

1. To prepare the fabric, cut the shapes including a ⅜″ seam allowance, using templates. You can use a plastic template made from the pattern, but it is even easier to use a commercial acrylic template. The fast2cut HexEssentials Viewers allow you to view the fabric placement for fussy-cutting scraps and to trim blocks from strips.

To cut geometric shapes from a strip, place the template on a strip that matches the outer dimensions of the template. Cut the 2 edges on the right and leave the template in place.

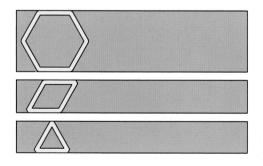

While the template is still in place, align a second ruler with a straight edge on the other side of the template. Move the template slightly and cut along the second ruler. If you need to cut more than 1 edge, move the template back into position so you can realign the second ruler with another edge, then move the template and cut the remaining edge.

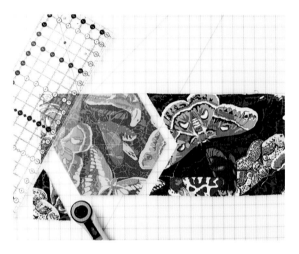

To cut geometric shapes from scraps, or even to finish trimming shapes cut from strips, it is really handy to use a rotating cutting mat. Center the template on the fabric and cut the first edge, then rotate the mat into position for making the next cut.

2. Next, use a paper template the exact size of the finished hexagon. I recommend commercial papers for most shapes and sizes, but you can make your own by tracing the patterns provided or use the HexEssentials viewing windows. Center the paper template on the back of the cut fabric shape. Run the fabric glue stick around the outer edge of the paper. Fold the fabric over the paper edge and finger-press. If you choose to baste, run the needle through the folds of the fabric and knot in place. No need to sew through the paper.

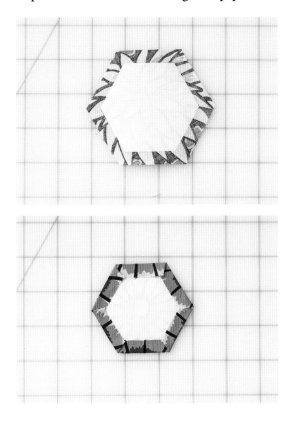

3. Place 2 hexagons from Step 2 right sides together, with flat edges aligned. You can whip-stitch across the entire edge, but I prefer to whipstitch just the first few stitches, then lay the shapes flat, right side down, and join the fabric by catching a small bit of the fabric near the right hexagon with the needle, running over the join, and then catching a small bit on the left hexagon. By working under the fabric in this manner, you can hide the stitch even more. Secure the thread.

4. Keep the paper inside the fabric shape until you have joined other pieces to all of its sides. Then *gently* slip your finger under the seam allowance to release the glue and remove the paper. If a shape is on the outside edge of a unit, use spray starch on the paper side while the paper is still attached, flip over, press, and let it cool. Gently remove the paper by sliding your finger under the fabric right before you sew the unit into the quilt. Most papers can be reused.

Appliqué

In keeping with my *Mixing Quilt Elements* theme, I used several appliqué techniques throughout the projects. In some projects, I turned edges by hand, as in traditional needle-turn appliqué. In others I used freezer paper, card stock, Mylar templates, or even a raw-edge appliqué technique. In addition to hand-stitching, several machine stitches work nicely for sewing the appliqué shapes to the background fabric. I encourage you to expand your repertoire of skills by exploring new techniques and finding the one (or more) that will work best for your project.

PREPARING APPLIQUÉ SHAPES

To make appliqué shapes, I trace the appliqué design onto freezer paper, then cut out the shape. Next, iron the freezer paper to the right side of the fabric. The next step is to trace the appliqué shape with a Bohin chalk pencil and remove the freezer paper. Cut out the shape, adding a ¼″ seam allowance around the chalk line. Turn the fabric from the inside edge of the chalk line to the back and finger-press in place. This method makes turning the fabric to the wrong side much easier. To test placement, I use a fabric glue stick lightly on the back of the shapes to position them until I am sure that I am happy.

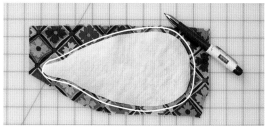

Trace the appliqué design onto freezer paper. Cut the shape on the line. Iron onto the right sides of your chosen fabrics. Trace around with a chalk pencil and remove the paper. Cut the shape with a ¼″ seam allowance and finger-press the excess to the back along the chalk line. Pin in place.

PREPARING APPLIQUÉ CIRCLES

One of my favorite ways to prepare appliqué circles is to baste the fabric around a template and press well with spray starch.

1. Cut the fabric circle ½″ larger than the finished size of the circle.

2. Baste around the edge of the circle with small stitches. Do not tie off.

3. Use a card stock or Mylar template in the exact size required for the finished circle. Place the template on the wrong side of the fabric and draw the thread up to bring the seam allowance around to the back. Smooth out the gathers around the edge of the circle. Check the front of the circle to be sure the outer edge is smooth.

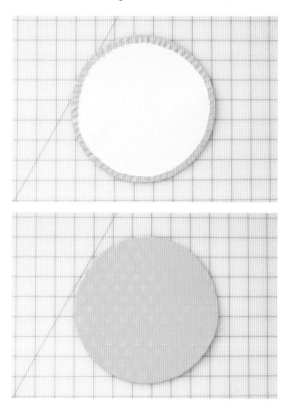

4. Press with a hot iron and spray starch. When the fabric has cooled, loosen the basting stitches and gently remove the template.

Alternatively, you could place the fabric right side down on a square of foil. Fold the edges of the foil over the back of the template and finger-press firmly in place. Press with a hot iron. The foil will hold the fabric in place and the heat creates a great crease for appliqué. Be sure to let it cool before removing the foil!

Making Bias Strips

Making bias strips is easy and fun. Cut long strips across the bias of a fat quarter. Using a long ruler, cut a strip ½″ wider than the desired finished width. Take this strip to the ironing board and spray with spray starch. With the wrong side up, fold the fabric and press a seam allowance down. Now flip the pressed bit toward the wrong side of the fabric and press again. When the stem has two sides pressed to the wrong side, cut the stem length needed. Repeat as many times as necessary. Vary the width if you'd like.

It is also possible to curve the stems by holding one end with the iron and then adding spray starch. Curve the stem by gently pulling in one direction and pressing until dry.

Bias strips can also be made using a commercial bias tape maker. Use the instructions that come with your bias tape maker to produce the folded bias strips needed for your projects.

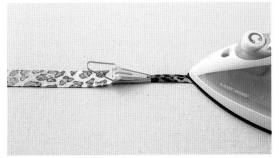

Use a ½″ bias tape maker to turn 1″ bias strips into bias stems.

CHECK OUT YOUR LOCAL QUILT SHOPS

Search for a local quilt shop that offers the opportunity to gather among a community of quilters. Ask questions about what you don't know. A good shop will be happy to help you find what you want! Quilt shops are critical for keeping the spirit of the patchwork community alive. Gather, sew, share ideas, and most of all, enjoy!

GO SLOWLY!

For more than two decades I have gathered fabrics, cut them, and sewn them together impulsively—driven by the need to make and make fast. Immediate satisfaction was a driving force in all my projects.

Now, at last, I have fallen in love with the slower methods of appliqué and English paper piecing as a way of using my hands while my mind sifts through the events of the day or when gathered with friends to stitch. Portable, quiet, and full of rewarding surprises, hand piecing has become a favorite method. I still enjoy making a quilt in a weekend, but discovering the slower methods has revealed a more thoughtful side of life. Hardly a day goes by without the needle and thread in my hand, working on projects that develop slowly over time and like a deep breath keep me in the present ... looking forward.

CHOOSING FABRICS

CENTER STAR DIAMONDS AND OUTSIDE STAR POINTS   Each diamond started with a feature fabric to be used in the 2½″ hexagon center. I felt an exciting rush as I moved the template around the fabric to find just the right motif. I then took them on the road and sewed during my travels before deciding on the layout upon returning home.

SETTING DIAMONDS   The setting diamonds are made with a variety of neutral prints ranging from white to off-white. I used whatever I had on hand and used the red center diamond to give it focus.

SETTING TRIANGLES   I always buy a large quantity when I find a feature fabric with drama and a dynamic palette, such as the very special green floral designed by Jennifer Paganelli. I had it in my stash and loved it, so I used it!

NEW STAR

FINISHED QUILT: 89½″ × 92″ (227 cm × 234 cm)

New Star represents the concept of mixing elements more than any other quilt in this book! The fabrics are dynamic prints and strong in color, but the star is set on the modern, low-volume background. The techniques include paper piecing, appliqué, and machine piecing.

One of the things I love about patchwork is the resourceful nature that is intrinsically a part of the process. Rather than cutting up our clothes or using scrap fabrics as in the old days, we now generally choose from a wide range of textile options. In some ways I miss the opportunity to make do, so I build an element of chance into my quilts by making suitable fabric substitutions or trying a new technique to achieve a desired result.

New Star started out as a pile of fabric with 2½″ hexagons, diamonds, and triangles for a take-away travel project. Upon returning, I had the diamonds complete and set about finding a layout for them. The trick was how to join the hand-pieced elements to the larger shapes required to make the star. It was a light-bulb moment when I realized I could make large diamond and triangle templates from cereal boxes, which were just the right strength for the oversized shapes!

For the inner border, I was torn between two colors for the stripe. I liked them both, so I chose to combine them—not because I didn't have enough but because I quietly enjoyed suggesting that by using two fabrics.

I always opt for machine piecing where it is possible; for example, in the border. Why hand piece when it is so easily done on the machine? However, with the assembly of the star, the hand piecing finished it neatly, accurately, and easily. I have enjoyed accruing enough skills to assess which one is best in any situation. Having said all this, if you like a quilt and choose a different way to make it, that choice is yours! Mix it up and have fun.

BACKGROUND The background had to be quiet. I selected two low-volume, equal-value prints from my stash, thinking along the popular modern trend.

INNER BORDER When it came to the stripes, I couldn't decide between the gold and red, so I used them both! I like the way it keeps the eye moving.

OUTER BORDER I happened to have the Amy Butler stripe on hand for the tips of the triangles, which works well with the two inner border stripes, extending their effect. The triangles used the remaining fabrics from many of the stars. It is a good design element to keep the same 60° shapes for the border.

BINDING I like a strong, striped binding. The fabric I used is a Kaffe Fassett paisley stripe, but any strong, dark stripe would do for a scrap quilt like this one.

MATERIALS

Yardage is based on 42"-wide (107 cm) fabric.

Star points and outer border:

- **Green floral:** 2¼ yards (2 m) for large triangles
- **Colorful prints:** A variety of strips that are at least 4½" × width of fabric (15 cm × width of fabric) for outer border triangle bases, plus a large supply of colorful fabrics for fussy cutting star diamonds, hexagons, and triangles. The largest scraps need to be approximately 6¼" × 6¼" (16 cm × 16 cm) for cutting the center hexagons.

Setting diamonds:

- **Red:** ⅛ yard (10 cm) for setting diamond centers
- **Neutrals:** ⅓ yard (25 cm) each of 6–8 fabrics for setting diamonds

Borders:

- **Red stripe:** ½ yard (50 cm) for inner border
- **Gold stripe:** ½ yard (50 cm) for inner border
- **Multicolored stripe:** ½ yard (50 cm) for triangle tips in outer border

Background:

- **Low-volume prints:** 2⅛ yards (2 m) each of 2 equal values for backgrounds
- **Binding:** ¾ yard (70 cm)
- **Backing:** 8¼ yards (7½ m)
- **Batting:** 98" × 100" (2.5 m × 2.5 m)

Tools and notions:

- **Card stock**
- **Fabric glue stick**
- **Milliners needles:** size 11
- **English paper-piecing papers:** 2½" hexagons, diamonds, and triangles
- *Optional:* fast2cut HexEssentials 2½" Viewers (by C&T Publishing)

CUTTING

All measurements include the seam allowance.

Refer to Favorite Techniques (page 17) for information about cutting strips, triangles, and hexagons. Prepare templates from the New Star patterns A–K/Kr (pullout page P2). Use card stock to prepare F and G templates. You may use commercial templates or specialty rulers for some of the cutting. Label the pieces.

Colorful scraps for star diamonds:

The star diamonds are fun to make using the best decorative aspects of fabric available today. Working on each diamond one at a time, select a group of 4 fabrics that work together but don't necessarily match. Quirky combinations are more interesting than obviously matched combinations of very similar or range fabrics. Remember when selecting fabrics to consider a range of value, hue, and graphic size and to use stripes, polka dots, or plaids as well as motif fabrics.

Use templates A, B, and C. You can use a commercial 2½″ hexagon template for A.

For each star diamond:

- Cut 1 set of pieces with 1 hexagon (A) from first fabric, 2 triangles (B) from the second fabric, and 6 diamonds from each of remaining 2 fabrics (C1 and C2). Keep this set of pieces together for 1 star diamond. Continue cutting pieces in sets to complete 12 star diamonds.

From the remaining colorful fabrics:

- Cut strips 4½″ × width of fabric as needed; subcut 32 shapes (J), using template J or a 60° ruler, by positioning 8½″ ruler line at base of each strip and cutting along edges of ruler for outside border.

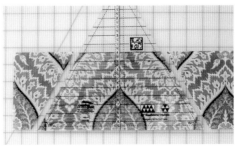

Cut the J shape with a template or a 60° ruler.

Neutral fabrics for setting diamonds:

- Using template D or a 22½° wedge ruler, cut the following wedge lengths. Cut wedges for 6 setting diamonds units.

For each setting diamond unit:
- Cut 6 wedges 9″ (36 total).
- Cut 4 wedges 6″ (24 total).
- Cut 6 wedges 5″ (36 total).

Green floral:

- Cut 2 strips 9¼″ × width of fabric; subcut 12 triangles (E), using template E or a 60° triangle ruler, for star point base triangles.

- Cut 6 strips 8½″ × width of fabric; subcut 36 triangles (I), using template I or a 60° triangle ruler, for outside border.

Multicolored stripe:

- Cut 3 strips 4½″ × width of fabric; subcut 32 triangles (H), using template H, for outside border. This template has a blunt tip, allowing the triangles to be cut from 4½″ strips. If your ruler does not, adjust your ruler to allow for the flat tip.

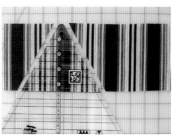
Cut 60° triangles with template H.

Red fabric for setting diamonds:

- Cut 6 diamonds (C) using template C.

Each background fabric:

- Cut 7 strips 9¼″ × width of fabric from each fabric (14 strips total).

Gold stripe fabric:

- Cut 4 strips 3¾″ × width of fabric.

Red stripe fabric:

- Cut 4 strips 3¾″ × width of fabric.

Binding fabric:

- Cut 10 strips 2½″ × width of fabric.

SEWING

All seam allowances are ¼", unless otherwise noted.

Pieced Diamonds

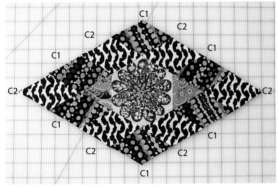

Make the pieced diamonds with 2½" hexagons, triangles, and diamonds.

Refer to English Paper Piecing (page 20) for more information about how to prepare the hexagons, triangles, and diamonds and how to sew them together.

1. For each pieced diamond, use a star diamond set (1 A hexagon, 2 B triangles, 2 sets of 6 C diamonds from your chosen fabrics).

2. Join a B triangle to 2 opposite sides of the center A hexagon.

3. Referring to the pieced star photo, arrange the C diamonds around the outer edge of the unit from Step 2, alternating the C diamond fabrics.

4. Join 2 sets of 2 C diamonds. Join to opposite sides of each pieced center diamond.

5. Join 4 C diamonds each for the 2 remaining sides of the center unit. Stitch them to the unit from Step 4.

6. Repeat Steps 1–5 to make 12 pieced diamonds. Set aside.

Setting Diamonds

Wedges are machine sewn, and red diamond is hand-appliquéd in center.

The wedges of the setting diamonds are machine sewn together using a ¼" seam.

1. For each setting diamond, use the following D wedges:

- 6 wedges 9" long
- 4 wedges 6" long
- 6 wedges 5" long

2. Arrange the wedges, matching narrow ends toward the center.

- Place 2 sets of 3 long wedges to be opposite points of the diamond.
- Place 2 sets of 3 short wedges to be opposite points perpendicular to the long wedges for the diamond.
- Place a medium-length wedge between each group of wedges to complete the diamond shape.

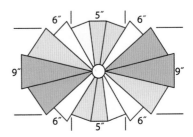

3. Starting with a long center wedge and working around the unit in a clockwise direction, machine-stitch the wedges together in pairs from the center out.

4. Keep working around the circle in a clockwise direction, sewing units together in pairs until all 16 wedges are joined into 1 unit. Press all the seams in the same direction. The raw center edges of the wedges will not join together.

5. Prepare 1 red C diamond as if for English paper piecing (page 20). Appliqué the red diamond to the center of the setting diamond. Gently release the seam allowance and remove the paper through the hole in the center of the block.

6. Repeat Steps 1–5 to make a total of 6 setting diamond units.

7. Make 6 card stock F templates, using the large diamond pattern F (pullout page P2), or draw your own diamonds using a 60° ruler. The diamonds should be 17⅜″ in length with each side measuring 10″.

8. Center a card stock diamond template F on the wrong side of a pieced setting diamond unit. Leaving a ¼″ seam allowance all around the card stock, trim away the excess fabric with a ruler and rotary cutter.

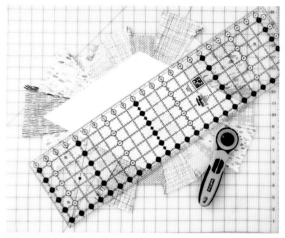

Trim to allow ¼″ seam allowance beyond card stock template.

9. Run a fabric glue stick or pen around the edge of the card stock template. Fold the seam allowance over to the back and finger-press in place.

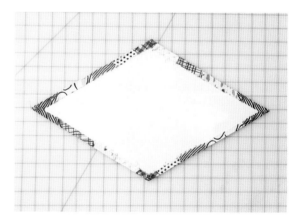

10. Repeat Steps 8 and 9 for all 6 setting diamonds. Set aside.

Star Assembly

1. Arrange 6 of the pieced diamonds together to form a 6-pointed center star. Hand stitch the diamonds together in pairs. Join the pairs together to complete the star.

2. In the same way you sewed smaller English paper-pieced shapes together, stitch a setting diamond between the star points to create a large, pieced hexagon. When this step is completed, you may take the papers out of the English paper-pieced diamonds, but leave the large card stock templates in the setting diamonds in place.

3. Use pattern G (the shaded area of pattern F) to make 2 card stock templates. You can use a 60° ruler to cut 2 card stock triangles with 10″ sides.

4. Center the card stock triangle templates on the back of 2 green floral E triangles. Run a glue stick or pen around the edge of each of each template. Fold the seam allowances to the back and finger-press in place.

5. Join the 2 green floral E triangles to 2 adjacent sides of a pieced diamond to create a large star point. Join the star point to a side of the center hexagon.

6. Using spray starch, press to crease the seam allowances in place. Gently run your finger under the unsewn seam allowances to remove the large card stock triangle templates from the floral green triangles.

7. Reuse the card stock triangle templates to prepare 2 more green floral E triangles. Repeat Steps 4–6 until you have completed the star.

Background Assembly

1. Join the 9¼″ background strips end to end, alternating between the 2 fabrics.

2. Subcut 8 strips 68″ long.

3. Sew the strips together to make a background 68″ × 70½″.

Appliquéing the Star

1. Fold the background into quarters and press at the folds.

2. Using spray starch, press the edges of the star. Remove the cardstock from all the diamonds and triangles except for the ones on the outer edge.

3. Position the star so the horizontal seams of the star align with the seams of the background, with the star points about 4″ from the edge of the background. The top and bottom star points rest on the vertical pressed marks of the background. Smooth out the star and pin in place.

4. Baste the star in place, removing the remaining papers as you go.

5. Appliqué the star to the background. Trim away the background fabric behind the star when the star is securely in place. Press flat.

Inner Border

1. Join a red 3¾″ strip to a gold 3¾″ strip for the inner border. Make 4 red/gold strips.

2. Measuring 34″ from the center seam of the strips in each direction, trim 2 red/gold strips to 2¾″ × 68″. Refer to the quilt photo to note the orientation of the red and gold to the quilt center. Pin the strips to the top and bottom of the quilt center, matching the center and ends of the quilt top to the center and ends of the striped strip. Sew in place.

3. Measuring 38½″ from the center seam of the strips in each direction, trim 2 red/gold strips to 2¾″ × 77″. Pin the strips to the sides of the quilt center, matching the center and ends of the quilt top to the center and ends of the striped strip. Sew in place.

Outer Borders

PIECED TRIANGLES

1. Sew a striped H triangle to a colorful print J triangle base to create a pieced triangle. Make 32 pieced triangles.

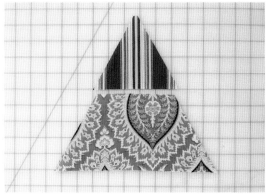

Position the tip over the base and join with a ¼″ seam.

2. To make the pieced half-triangles at the ends of each border, sew a striped 4½″ × width-of-fabric strip and a colorful print 4½″ × width-of-fabric strip together. Use the K/Kr template or a 60° ruler to cut 4 K half-triangles and 4 Kr half-triangles.

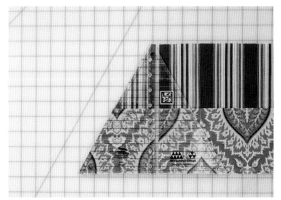

Join 2 strips and use the 60° ruler to cut 4 K half-triangles and 4 Kr half-triangles for the ends of outer borders.

OUTER BORDER ASSEMBLY

1. To make the top and bottom borders, alternate and join 7 pieced border triangles and 8 large green floral I triangles. Add a pieced K or Kr half-triangle at each end. Repeat to make 2 border strips. Matching the tip of the center outer border triangle with the center seam of the inner border, pin at the strip center and the ends. Sew a border strip to the top and the bottom of the quilt.

2. To make the side borders, alternate and join 9 pieced border triangles and 10 large green floral I triangles. Add a pieced K or Kr half-triangle at each end. Repeat to make 2 border strips. Matching the tip of the center outer border triangle with the center seam of the inner border, pin at the strip center and the ends. Sew a border strip to each side of the quilt.

QUILTING

This quilt was custom quilted by Jan Foster of Red Shed Quilting. We discussed the lines of the quilt and where I wanted detail or just fill. She did an incredible job of accenting the quilt with great detail and just the perfect amount of quilting!

LOVE BIRDS

FINISHED QUILT: 84½″ × 84½″ (215 cm × 215 cm) ■ **FINISHED BLOCK:** 20″ × 20″ (51 cm × 51 cm)

Images of summer fans and whimsical folk art–inspired appliqué are brought to life here with my trusty favorite tool, the wedge ruler, and a bundle of happy contemporary fabrics including those by Kaffe Fassett, Anna Maria Horner, and Amy Butler. Wedges add so much interest to a quilt with their curved edges and the endless possibilities of exciting fabric combinations.

In this quilt I imagine my memories of cattails and ducks that filled the ponds of my youth and add the color of the chatting birds that squawk in the trees outside my studio window today. Simple shapes, simply made, fill the blocks. Add a few hexagons and a variety of techniques, and the quilt is complete.

The appliqué is all needle-turn; however, you can adjust the pattern for machine appliqué using blanket stitch and/or fusible web if you prefer.

CHOOSING FABRICS

WEDGES   Make your wedge fans first. Select wedges in pairs of print fabrics that have strong graphics and colors to pair with polka dots. The leftover scraps will come in handy for your hexagons and appliqué.

BORDER   The pastel stripes work nicely to consolidate the palette of the quilt and add just a bit of graphic energy.

HEXAGONS   These are made with a random collection of scrap fabrics. Anything will do.

APPLIQUÉ   Consider mixing warm and cool colors within the pattern so that the contrast adds zest to your blocks. Use as many extra scraps as you like and feel free to add in personal ideas anywhere. For the backgrounds, look for prints that have a regular-sized spot repeat, which will read more like a neutral than a print with irregularly sized or spaced spots. Make it more country with plaids or simplify with homespun colors.

MATERIALS

Yardage is based on 42"-wide (107 cm) fabric.

- **Multicolored stripe:** 2½ yards (2.3 m) for striped border

Light backgrounds with:

- **Pink dots:** 1¼ yards (1.2 m)
- **Pea green dots:** 1¼ yards (1.2 m)
- **Light blue dots:** 1¼ yards (1.2 m)
- **Yellow dots:** 2 yards (1.8 m)

Fans:

- **Red:** ¼ yard (20 cm) for 3½" circle centers
- **Colorful prints:** ⅓ yard (25 cm) each of 16 fabrics
- **Polka dots:** ⅓ yard (25 cm) each of 8–16 fabrics

Appliqué:

- **Green/brown prints:** 4 fat quarters for stems
- **Assorted fabrics:** 2 yards of scraps in a variety of colors, keeping in mind these appliqué figures: diamonds for flowers, birds, flower pot, leaves, and hexagons
- **Binding:** ¾ yard (70 cm)
- **Backing:** 7¾ yards (7 m)
- **Batting:** 93" × 93" (2.3 m × 2.3 m)

Tools and notions:

- **Milliners needles:** size 11
- **Thread:** Aurifil 50-weight thread in a neutral color or to match each appliqué fabric
- **Spray starch:** such as Mary Ellen's Best Press spray starch alternative
- **Templates:** 3½" and 1" circle templates, or use your own templates made from *Love Birds* patterns B and E (pullout page P1)
- **Chalk pencil**

- **Appliqué pins**
- **Freezer paper**
- **English paper-piecing papers:** ⅝" hexagons (180)
- **English paper-piecing papers:** 1½" diamonds (24) *or* your own templates made from *Love Birds* pattern D (pullout page P1)
- *Optional:* 18° wedge ruler
- *Optional:* fast2cut HexEssentials Small Viewers (by C&T Publishing)

CUTTING

Refer to Favorite Techniques (page 17) for information about cutting strips, wedges, hexagons, and appliqué shapes. All measurements include the seam allowance for patterns A–E. Seam allowances are not included on patterns F–S. Prepare templates from the Love Birds *patterns A–S (pullout page P1) or use commercial templates or specialty rulers for some pieces (as listed in Tools and Notions). Label the pieces.*

Fan fabrics:

Cut 16 sets of wedges, keeping the sets separate.

For each set of fans:

- Cut 4 wedges (A) from polka dot fabric, using template A or 18° wedge ruler.
- Cut 6 wedges (A) from 1 print, using template A or 18° wedge ruler.

Background fabrics:

- Cut 9 squares total 21″ × 21″ for blocks.
- Cut 4 squares 12½″ × 12½″ for border corners.

Border stripes:

- Cut 6 strips 12½″ × width of fabric; subcut 12 rectangles 12½″ × 20½″.

Red fabric:

- Cut 16 circles (B), using template B.

Assorted fabrics:

Refer to the quilt photo (page 43) for colors. Additional cutting will be done in the construction steps.

- Cut appliqué pieces for *Love Birds* patterns F–S (pullout page P1), referring to Appliqué (page 22) for information about cutting and preparing appliqué shapes.
- Cut 1 bias strip 1″ diagonally across the widest section of each green/brown print fat quarter. If you need more strips for stems later, you can cut them when you lay out your appliqué blocks.
- Cut 24 diamonds (D) using template D.
- Cut 180 hexagons (C) using template C or fast2cut HexEssentials ⅝″ Viewer.

Binding fabric:

- Cut 9 strips 2½″ × width of fabric.

SEWING

All seam allowances are ¼″, unless otherwise noted.

Fans

1. From 1 set of fan wedges, join 2 polka dot wedges and 3 print wedges, alternating fabrics, to make a fan. Make a second identical fan from the remaining wedges in the set. Repeat with the remaining sets of wedges to make a total of 16 pairs of fans.

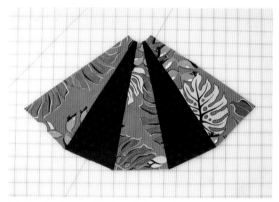

Join 2 polka dots and 3 prints. Make a pair of fans from each fabric combination.

2. Referring to the quilt assembly diagram (page 43), arrange the 9 background squares and the border rectangles and corner squares on your design wall. Lay out the fans in pairs according to the diagram, making sure the colors vary throughout in value and hue. If you are having trouble getting a good balance of colors, another option is to randomly place the fans without putting them in pairs.

> **tip**
>
> *To remember how you arranged the colors, take a quick snapshot of the quilt layout. Refer to the photo when you are ready to assemble the quilt.*

3. Work on 1 fan background square at a time. These 21″ × 21″ squares are ½″ oversized to allow for some shrinkage during appliqué. Mark the finished size (20″ × 20″) with a pencil before starting to avoid working outside the finished size. Fold the background 21″ fan square in half vertically and horizontally. Press the folds, then open the square and place it faceup on a flat surface.

4. Finger-press a ¼″ seam allowance into the outer curve of the fan. Position the fan in a quarter of the background square, allowing the 2 straight edges of the fans to extend beyond the pencil lines, and pin in place. Use a neutral thread to appliqué the fan in place.

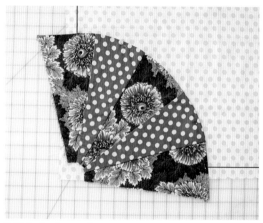

Fold the background into quarters and fold the fans in half. Match the folds and pin the fan in place.

5. Repeat Steps 4 and 5 to appliqué fans in the remaining quarters of the block. With a straight ruler, trim the block to 20½″ × 20½″. Repeat to make a total of 5 blocks.

6. Using the same technique, appliqué 2 fans to the border stripe 12½″ × 20½″ rectangle for the center of each border and 1 fan to each border corner 12½″ × 12½″ square, following the color arrangement you planned in Step 2.

Hexagons

Refer to English Paper Piecing (page 20) for more information about how to prepare the hexagons and sew them together.

Hexagon unit

1. Join a row of 6 hexagons.

2. Add a row of 5 hexagons on either side of the first row.

3. Add a row of 4 hexagons on either side.

4. Add a row of 3 hexagons on either side.

5. Add 2 hexagons on either side.

6. Add 1 hexagon on either side to complete the unit.

7. Repeat Steps 1–6 to make 4 more hexagon units (5 total).

8. Position a hexagon unit in the center of each fan block in the quilt body. Remove the papers from the center of the hexagon and pin in place. Gently appliqué around the shape. Remove the outer papers as you go.

Appliqué Blocks

Refer to Appliqué (page 22).

1. Fold the backgrounds for the 21″ × 21″ appliqué blocks in half vertically and horizontally and press to mark guidelines. These squares are ½″ oversized to allow for some shrinkage during appliqué. Mark the finished size (20″ × 20″) with a pencil before starting to avoid working outside the finished size. Set aside.

2. Refer to English Paper Piecing (page 20) for information to prepare 24 D diamonds. Refer to the Block 3 diagram (page 42) to see the star flowers. Make 4 star flowers for block 3, using 6 D diamonds for petals in each flower.

- Use 24 commercial diamond papers or make your own from *Love Birds* pattern D (pullout page P1). Place each diamond paper on the back of a fabric diamond and glue the seam allowance to the back of the paper. Join the diamonds in sets of 6 to make 4 flowers. Press with spray starch.

- Make a 1″ circle template from card stock, using *Love Birds* pattern E. Refer to Preparing Appliqué Circles (page 22) to make 4 yellow circles.

- Appliqué the yellow centers to the flower centers. Remove the diamond papers just before you are ready to appliqué.

3. Use a ½″ bias tape maker to turn under the edges of the 1″ bias strips in the green/brown prints. See Making Bias Strips (page 23).

4. Prepare the remaining appliqué pieces. Start with the top layers first. For example, to get the birds ready to be placed on the background fabric, compose them by appliquéing the wings, eyes, and beaks in place.

5. When the appliqué shapes are complete, position them in place on the backgrounds. Refer to the quilt photo (next page) as well as the block diagrams. These blocks are simple and free form. Position your shapes as you like or change the layout to one that pleases your eye. Pin or baste in place.

6. Needle-turn appliqué the shapes to the background, using a fine, neutral appliqué thread like Aurifil 50-weight in gray, or a thread that matches the color of the appliqué shape. Once the blocks are complete, trim the blocks to 20½″ × 20½″.

Block 1: Flower (F), bird (G), vase (H), leaf (L)

Block 2: Heart (I), leaf (J), leaf (K), leaf (L)

Block 3: Leaf (M), flower center (N), bird (O), bird (P)

Block 4: Big bird (Q), half bird (R), cattail (S)

HOW TO NEEDLE-TURN APPLIQUÉ

1. Finger-press all curved seams.

2. Use the needle to sweep the seam allowance under to the chalk line.

3. Sew with tiny appliqué stitches. Bring the needle up through the background from behind the appliqué piece. This way, the thread end will not show through the background. Come up through the fold of the finger-pressed line along the appliqué shape. Take the needle straight back down through the background directly under the entry point. Go along no more than ⅛″ behind the fabric and come out in the fold of the fabric again. Pull the thread through with a slight tug so the shape lies flat, but not so much that it gathers the edge.

STITCHING CURVES For convex (outward) curves, just turn the seam allowance under, being careful to smooth out any tucks to avoid points in the curves. For concave (inward) curves, trim the seam allowance to about ⅛″ and clip the seam allowance at tight curves so it can lie flat under the shape. Use shorter appliqué stitches to secure the fabric.

STITCHING POINTS For outward points, stitch up to the marked line at the corner, then trim the allowance if needed and use the needle to push the next seam allowance under to the marked line. Gently tug the thread and continue sewing around the other side.

Red Circles

Refer to Preparing Appliqué Circles (page 22). Prepare the 16 B circles for appliqué. Set aside.

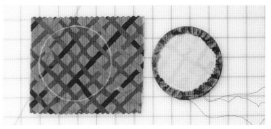

Trace the circle with a chalk pencil and cut out with a ¼″ seam allowance.

Quilt Assembly

1. Following the color placement plan you made while working on the fan blocks, lay out the 9 center blocks and border pieces.

2. Sew the quilt body together in 3 rows of 3 blocks each.

3. Sew a plain stripe border rectangle to each end of a border fan rectangle. Repeat to make a total of 4 border units.

4. Sew a border unit to both sides of the quilt, matching the border seamlines with the block seamlines.

5. Sew a corner fan block to each end of the 2 remaining border units, paying attention to the direction of the fans. Sew these to the top and bottom of the quilt, matching seamlines.

6. Position the red circles over the intersections between fan pairs throughout the quilt. Pin and appliqué in place.

QUILTING

Love Birds was machine quilted by Bhijan Attwell, who stitched in the ditch to stabilize the quilt. Then I went back with perle cotton #8 and quilted around the appliqué, along the stripes in the border, and around the hexagons for a bit of extra decoration.

Quilt assembly

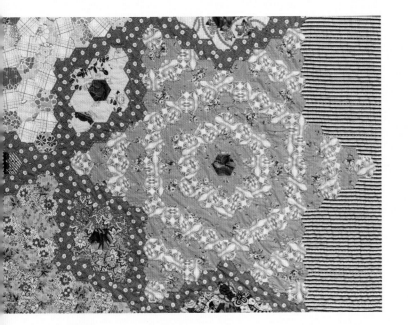

HOPE HAMMOCK

FINISHED QUILT: 87½″ × 96″ (222 cm × 244 cm)

*Quilting is a source of strength for me. I never would have dreamed I had the fortitude to do an entire quilt by hand. I commenced **Hope Hammock** without a moment's hesitation the day I learned I had breast cancer. I wrote a blog post the night before I went into surgery. In the morning I woke to find more than 300 emails offering support and love from friends and strangers alike. I imagined a hammock of fingers holding me safe throughout my experience. It took me two years to complete the hexagons and hand quilting, all the while supported by kindness.*

CHOOSING FABRICS

STARS The fabrics were chosen in pairs entirely from my stash with nothing more than a vague idea of how I wanted it to turn out. It was a chance to do something pretty … not normal for me!

STAR CENTERS I used a strong red Kaffe Fassett for the star centers for a focus point.

SETTING DIAMONDS The setting diamonds are outlined in a light brown fabric that gracefully lends importance to the soft stars. The idea here is to choose a neutral fabric with a touch of texture.

BORDER The stripe border has an equal weight but different texture from the setting diamonds.

BINDING The binding carries on in the same soft brown but with a polka dot instead of a stripe. The texture variation is blended by the similar value of the fabrics.

To be honest, I never labor too hard over these decisions. The urge to get going is stronger than the urge to fuss, so I just start sewing. If you are more careful by nature, you can make up a few rounds of stars. Let them sit for a while on the design wall until you feel comfortable.

MATERIALS

Yardage is based on 42"-wide (107 cm) fabric.

- **Red:** ⅜ yard (35 cm) for centers of stars and setting diamonds
- **Prints:**

    ⅝ yard (60 cm) each of 2 contrasting prints for each of 8 stars (16 total)

    ⅜ yard (35 cm) each of 2 contrasting prints for each of 2 half-stars (4 total)

    ⅛ yard (10 cm) each of 23 prints for inner row of setting diamonds
- **Light brown:** 2¾ yards (2.5 m) for outer rows of setting diamonds
- **Stripe:** 2⅞ yards (2.6 m) for border
- **Binding:** ¾ yard (70 cm)
- **Backing:** 8 yards (7.3 m)
- **Batting:** 96" × 104" (2.4 m × 2.6 m)

Tools and notions:

- **Milliners needles:** size 11
- **Thread:** Aurifil 50-weight cotton thread in a neutral color
- **Fabric glue stick and refills**
- **English paper-piecing papers:** 1¼" hexagons (1,650)
- *Optional:* 1¼" hexagon template for rotary cutting (really handy)
- *Optional:* Rotating rotary-cutting mat (Rotating mats are great for trimming hexagons.)

CUTTING

All measurements include the seam allowance.

Refer to Favorite Techniques (page 17) for information about cutting strips and hexagons. The hexagons for the stars and diamonds are not fussy cut, but rather cut from strips using a rotary cutter. Prepare a template from the Hope Hammock *pattern (pullout page P2). Cut all hexagons using this template.*

Red:

- Cut 3 strips 3″ × width of fabric; subcut 33 total hexagons (10 for stars and half-stars; 23 for setting diamonds and half-setting diamonds).

2 contrasting prints for each whole star:

- From print 1, cut 6 strips 3″ × width of fabric; subcut 60 hexagons for rounds 1, 3, 5, and 7.
- From print 2, cut 6 strips 3″ × width of fabric; subcut 60 hexagons for rounds 2, 4, 6, and 8.

2 contrasting prints for each half-star:

- From print 1, cut 3 strips 3″ × width of fabric from each fabric; subcut 30 hexagons for rounds 1, 3, 5, and 7.
- From print 2, cut 3 strips 3″ × width of fabric from each fabric; subcut 34 hexagons for rounds 2, 4, 6, and 8.

23 prints for setting diamonds:

- From 19 prints, cut 1 strip 3″ × width of fabric; subcut 8 hexagons for center round in full-setting diamonds.
- From 5 remaining prints, cut 1 strip 3″ × width of fabric; subcut 5 hexagons for center round in half-setting diamonds.

Light brown fabric for setting diamonds:

- Cut 32 strips 3″ × width of fabric; subcut 344 hexagons for outer round in spacer units. Set aside 4 hexagons for border corners.

Border stripe:

- Cut 6 strips 12″ × width of fabric. Join strips end to end; subcut 2 strips 12″ × 104″.
- Cut 4 strips 4″ × width of fabric. Join strips end to end; subcut 2 strips 4″ × 78½″.

Binding fabric:

- Cut 10 strips 2½″ × width of fabric.

SEWING

All seam allowances are ¼", unless otherwise noted.

Hexagon Star and Half Star

See English Paper Piecing (page 20) for more information about preparing and sewing the hexagons.

1. To make a whole star, begin with the red center hexagon. For round 1, join hexagons of print 1 to all 6 sides of the red hexagon. Continue adding rounds until you have made 4 full rounds, alternating prints 1 and 2 from round to round.

Star center

2. Make a star point by joining 4 hexagons of print 1 (same print as round 1 of the star center). Add 3 hexagons of print 2, then 2 hexagons, then 1, as shown, alternating prints 1 and 2. Repeat to make a total of 6 star points.

Make 6 star points.

3. Join the star points to the outer edges of the star center, with one open space (the size of 1 hexagon) on the star center between the points. Study the diagram because this can get confusing. I did unpick a few!

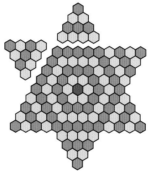

Star assembly

4. Repeat Steps 1–3 to make 8 full stars.

5. Referring to the half-star assembly diagram, use the same method to make 2 half-stars. Join 4 half-rounds of hexagons for the center. Make 2 full star points and 2 half-star points. Join the points to the center to complete the half-stars.

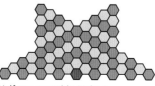

Half-star assembly. Make 2.

Setting Diamonds

1. Each setting diamond will have 1 red hexagon, 8 print hexagons, and 16 light brown hexagons. Starting with a red hexagon, make 1 round of a print fabric. Add a hexagon to 2 opposite ends. Round 2 has 14 light brown hexagons and another light brown hexagon at each end. Repeat to make a total of 19 setting diamonds.

Setting diamond assembly. Make 19.

2. To make a setting half-diamond, add a print hexagon to 3 adjacent sides of a red hexagon. Refer to the diagram to add 2 more print hexagons to the ends. For round 2, add 7 light brown hexagons, then add 1 more light brown hexagon to each end. Each half-setting diamond will have 1 red hexagon, 5 print hexagons, and 9 light brown hexagons. Repeat to make a total of 4 setting half-diamonds.

Half-diamond assembly. Make 4.

Quilt Assembly

1. Refer to the quilt assembly diagram to arrange the stars into 2 columns of 3 stars and a center column of 2 stars.

2. Start at the top and fill in the gaps between the stars with setting diamonds. Add the half-stars and half-setting diamonds to the top and bottom.

3. Remove all the hexagon papers except for the outer rows of the units.

4. Join the setting diamonds to each side of the center column of stars. In the outer columns, join the setting diamonds between each star.

5. Join an outer column of stars to each side of the center stars to complete the quilt center.

6. When the quilt center is complete, align the vertical center of the quilt center with the center of each 12″ × 104″ side border and pin. Then baste the quilt center to the side borders with the tips of the star points about 1½″ from the outside edge. Leave only the outside hexagon papers in place and remove them as you appliqué around the edge. Leave the corners open.

7. Appliqué the star body to the 4″-wide top and bottom borders with the hexagons about 1½″ from outside edge as you did the side borders.

8. Miter the corners by hand and appliqué the last 4 light brown hexagons in place over the seamline.

Here's my quilt in progress on my design wall. I placed the columns horizontally to give me more space to work, and played with the color placement of the stars before I started adding setting diamonds.

QUILTING

I hand quilted this quilt with cream perle cotton #8.

Quilt assembly

BABY OCTAGON

FINISHED QUILT: 31″ × 38″ (79 cm × 97 cm) ■ **FINISHED BLOCK:** Octagons and squares with 1″ sides

Solid fabrics, particularly these Modern Solids by Jason Yenter, are wonderful to work with and allow for all kinds of interesting palette stories. Mixed with the funky plaid by Art Gallery and an Alexander Henry polka dot, they really take on a life of their own in this little cot quilt project. It was one of the first English paper-pieced projects that I made, and as a result I'd say there are a few places where my stitches show too much. I can live with that!

CHOOSING FABRICS

OCTAGONS   Choose any color palette that you like for your octagons. Mine is typical of the heritage color scheme found in many heritage houses in Sydney.

SQUARES   The squares are a medium-sized black-on-white dot.

INNER BORDER   The plaid does the work of piecing by combining the colors used into a strong graphic print.

OUTER BORDER   Using the scraps from the strips cut for the octagons and more of the polka dot makes this border easy to make.

QUILTING   I used perle cotton #12 in black and tiny stitches throughout. Girl or boy? Doesn't matter, this graphic print will keep their baby eyes bouncing!

MATERIALS

Yardage is based on 42"-wide (107 cm) fabric.

- **Solids:** ⅛ yard (10 cm) each of 25 colors for octagons and outer border
- **Black-and-white polka dots:** ⅞ yard (80 cm) for setting squares and outer border
- **Plaid:** ¼ yard (25 cm) for inner border
- **Binding:** ⅜ yard (35 cm)
- **Backing:** 1⅜ yards (1.25 m)
- **Batting:** 39" × 46" (99 cm × 117 cm)

Tools and notions:

- **Milliners needles:** size 11
- **Thread:** Aurifil 50-weight cotton thread in a neutral color to blend with octagons
- **English paper-piecing papers:** 1" octagons (88) and 1" squares (108)
- *Optional:* Octagon Template Set (by Material Obsession)

CUTTING

All measurements include the seam allowance. Refer to Favorite Techniques (page 17) for information about cutting strips and octagons. Prepare templates from the Baby Octagon *patterns A–C (pullout page P2) or use commercial templates or specialty rulers. Label the pieces.*

Solid fabric for octagons:

- Cut 1 strip 3¼″ × width of fabric from each fabric; subcut 3–4 octagons (A), using template A.

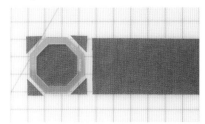

Cut 3–4 octagons from each strip.

- Sew remaining strip length together, matching the long sides to make striped fabric for the border triangles.
- Cut 2½″-wide strips perpendicular to the seams; subcut 58 triangles (C), using template C or a quarter-square triangle ruler for the outer border. If your ruler does not have a blunt tip at the top, refer to pattern C to mark it.

Black-and-white dot:

- Cut 5 strips 1¾″ × width of fabric; subcut 108 squares (B) 1¾″ × 1¾″, using template B.
- Cut 4 strips 2½″ × width of fabric; subcut 50 triangles (C), using template C, for border.
- Cut 4 squares 4½″ × 4½″ for outer border corners.
- Cut 4 squares 2⅞″ × 2⅞″; subcut each square diagonally once to yield 8 half-square triangles to use at ends of each outer border strip.

Plaid:

Check the width and length of your quilt before you cut the border strips.

- Cut 3 strips 2″ × width of fabric; subcut 2 strips 2″ × 30½″ for inner side borders and 2 strips 2″ × 20″ for inner top and bottom borders.

Binding fabric:

- Cut 4 strips 2½″ × width of fabric.

SEWING

All seam allowances are ¼", unless otherwise noted.

Octagons

Refer to English Paper Piecing (page 20) for more information about how to prepare the octagons and squares and how to sew them together.

1. Use octagon and square papers to prepare the solid-color octagons and black-and-white squares for English paper piecing.

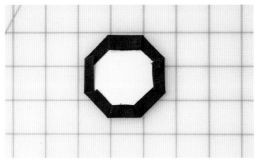

Glue-baste the seam allowances to the back of the octagon.

2. Join 2 octagons together along one flat side. Add a square and progress from top to bottom, adding octagons and setting squares. Vary the color combinations throughout.

Join 2 octagons.

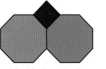

Add a black-and-white square between the octagons.

3. When you have completed 11 rows of 8 octagons each, open the seams on the outer octagons and press them flat. On the back of the quilt top, align a straight ruler with the tops of the octagons on the outer edge and mark with a chalk pencil or a felt-tip pen, whatever will show up on the back of the fabric. Wait to trim until you have sewn the inner borders to the quilt body.

Inner Border

1. Align the top and bottom borders with the line you marked on the outer edges of the octagons. Match the center of the border with the center of the quilt body. Attach the top and bottom borders to the quilt.

2. Trim the borders and the black-and-white squares even with the quilt center as needed. Trim the border ends even with the quilt center if needed.

3. Repeat Steps 1 and 2 to attach the inner side borders.

PIECED OUTER BORDER

1. Measure the width and length of your quilt body.

2. Join quarter-square strip-pieced triangles to black-and-white dot triangles in pairs and press flat. Join the pairs together until you have strips just a little longer than the length you need for each border. End each strip with a half-square triangle of the black-and-white dot.

- For the top and bottom borders, you will need 4 border strips that can be trimmed to approximately 23" long.

- For the side borders, you will need 4 border strips, that can be trimmed to approximately 30½" long.

3. For each border, align 2 similar-length border strips from Step 2 along the black-and-white dot fabrics, matching the center of each triangle with the center of the corresponding triangle in the other strip. Pin, then sew together with a ¼″ seam. Press the seams to one side. The black-and-white dot fabric triangles will form a zigzag effect, bordered by the pieced color triangles, as shown. Make border sections for the top, the bottom, and the sides of the quilt.

4. Trim each border strip to fit the quilt measurements.

Quilt Assembly

1. Match the centers and ends of the top and bottom border strips with the body of the quilt. Pin, then sew to the quilt body.

2. Join a 4½″ × 4½″ black-and-white dot square to each end of the side border strips. Match the centers and ends of a border triangle seam with the quilt body. Pin, then sew the borders to the quilt.

QUILTING

To quilt, I used black perle cotton #12 and quilted ¼″ inside the octagon columns. On the borders I echoed the triangle shapes.

Quilt assembly

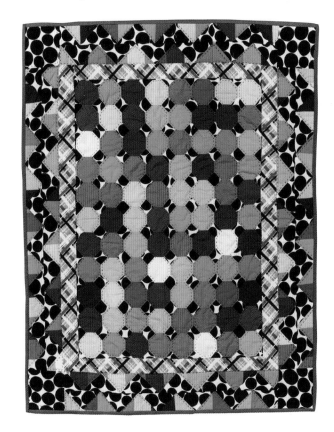

WEDGE WORK

Move over Dresden Plate; the wedge just got modern! No longer do we associate the wedge with only 1930s fabrics, even as well suited as they are. Wedge rulers of any size are zip lines to fun! Every time I pick one up I find something new to make. Circles, wedding rings, wild-shaped butterflies, even Log Cabins—all take on a new flair when made with a wedge. It is a tool handy to modern and traditional quilters and everything in between!

When you have enough fabric, this is the tool to get the stash working for you. Combine old and new, straight and curve, light and dark, or any combination you can think of for a new direction.

THE CHALLENGE

FINISHED QUILT: 51″ x 51″ (130 cm x 130 cm) ■ **FINISHED BLOCK:** 19″ x 19″ (48 cm x 48 cm)

*My quilts have been defined by the use of polychromatic, dramatic mixtures of texture and print with no limits. The idea of making a quilt with two colors, and one of them white, well, it just was **not** on my radar. Then I saw the red-and-white quilt exhibition in Houston, which reduced me to tears.*

The Challenge *for me was to not explore color at all, but simply pattern.*

I did, however, use one of my favorite tricks, and that was to mix two different neutrals in the background. English paper piecing, a 10° wedge, and an old-fashioned style of appliqué made ***The Challenge*** *a pleasure!*

Hand quilted with perle cotton #12 … a very surprisingly satisfying project.

CHOOSING FABRICS

FABRICS   Pick your red. For the white, use 2 shades of white, as I did, or simplify it to a single fabric. The very subtle difference adds just a bit of mystery or age to the project.

MATERIALS

Yardage is based on 42"-wide (107 cm) fabric.

- **Red:** 3⅛ yards (3 m)
- **Bright white:** 2⅝ yards (2.5 m)
- **Off-white:** 1⅛ yards (1 m)
- **Binding:** ½ yard (50 cm)
- **Backing:** 3¼ yards (3 m)
- **Batting:** 59" × 59" (150 cm × 150 cm)

Tools and notions:

- **Red and white cotton threads:** 40-weight for machine sewing and 50-weight for hand sewing
- **Milliners needles:** size 11
- **Fabric glue stick**
- **Marking pencil**
- **Card stock**
- **English paper-piecing papers:** ¾" hexagons (148)
- *Optional:* 2" and 6" circle templates
- *Optional:* 10° wedge ruler
- *Optional:* fast2cut HexEssentials Small Viewers (by C&T Publishing)

CUTTING

All measurements include the seam allowance.

Refer to Favorite Techniques (page 17) for information about cutting strips, wedges, and hexagons. Prepare templates for The Challenge *patterns A–G (pullout page P2). You may use specialty templates and rulers for some pieces (see the Material List). Label the pieces.*

Red:

- Cut 2 squares 20½″ × 20½″ for wheel block backgrounds.
- Cut 4 strips 6½″ × width of fabric; subcut 95 wedges (A), using template A or a 10° wedge ruler.
- Cut 8 strips 4½″ × width of fabric; subcut 8 strips 4½″ × 22½″ for outer border.

- Cut 5 strips 2⅛″ × width of fabric; subcut 74 hexagons, using template C or fast2cut HexEssentials ¾″ Viewer, for wheels and sashing.
- Cut 3 strips 2″ × width of fabric; subcut 44 circles (D), using template D.
- Cut 4 strips 1½″ × width of fabric; subcut 2 strips 1½″ × 24½″ and 2 strips 1½″ × 23½″ for sashing.

From remaining red fabric:
- Cut 2 diamonds (G), using template G, for border corners.
- Cut 2 triangles (F) and 2 reversed triangles (Fr), using template F/Fr, for each border corner edge.
- Cut 1 square 3¼″ × 3¼″.
- Cut 1 circle, using template B.

Bright white:

- Cut 2 squares 20½″ × 20½″ for wheel block backgrounds.
- Cut 5 strips 2⅛″ × width of fabric; cut 74 hexagons (C), using template C or fast2cut HexEssentials ¾″ Viewer, for wheels and sashing.
- Cut 8 strips 4½″ × width of fabric; subcut 8 strips 4½″ × 22½″ for outer border.
- Cut 4 strips 1½″ × width of fabric; subcut 2 strips 1½″ × 24½″ and 2 strips 1½″ × 23½″ for sashing.

- Cut 2 circles (D), using template D.
- Cut 2 diamonds (G), using template G, for border corners.
- Cut 2 triangles (F) and 2 reversed triangles (Fr), using template F/Fr, for each border corner edge.

Off-white:

- Cut 4 strips 6½″ × width of fabric; subcut 95 wedges (A), using template A or 10° wedge ruler.

Binding fabric:

- Cut 6 strips 2½″ × width of fabric.

SEWING

All seam allowances are ¼", unless otherwise noted.

Wheel Blocks

1. Join alternating red and off-white A wedges, narrow ends aligned, in sets of 36 to make 4 circles. Press all seams toward the red.

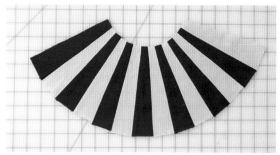

Join alternating red and off-white wedges in sets of 36 to make 4 complete wheels.

2. Fold each wedge circle into quarters and press the outer edges. Do the same for each background square. Right sides up, place a wedge circle on top of a background square, matching the folds. Pin the circle in place. Turn the outer edge of the circle under ¼" and appliqué to the background. Make 4. Set aside while you make the hexagon centers.

3. Refer to English Paper Piecing (page 20) for information about how to prepare and join the C hexagons. Set the prepared hexagons aside, in 2 sets with 18 of each color and 2 sets with 19 of each color.

4. Join the hexagons to make 2 of Hexagon Star A and 2 of Hexagon Star B.

Make 2 red A stars.   Make 2 white B stars.

5. Center the hexagon stars in the open center of a wedge circle. Pin, then appliqué in place. Hexagon Stars A, with the red star, go on the red backgrounds. Hexagon Stars B, with the white star, go on the white backgrounds.

6. Trim the blocks to 19½" × 19½", centering the wheel in the square.

Pieced Sashing

1. Join the remaining 23 red and 23 white A wedges, top and tail, alternating red and white, so they form a straight strip. Press toward the red wedges.

Keep tops and tails of the wedges even as you join them together.

2. Cut the strip in half through the length of the strip width to make 2 strips, each 3¼" × length of strip. One will be mostly red and the other mostly white. Set aside until you assemble the quilt top.

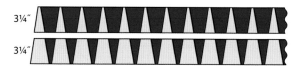

3. Cut each strip in half to yield 4 shorter strips.

Outer Borders

1. Using pieces G, F, and Fr, make 2 border corners with red centers and white edges and 2 border corners with white centers and red edges. Set aside while you make the border strips.

Make 2 of each.

2. With right sides facing up, align a red border strip with a white border strip. Stitch ¼″ from each long edge, using a basting stitch along one edge and a regular-length stitch along the other.

3. Align template E along the edge with the regular stitch length and use a pencil to trace triangles onto the red fabric. Leave a ¼″ gap below the basting stitches and make the traced lines intersect on the line of regular-length stitching as shown.

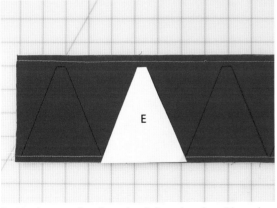

Position bottom edge of template E along the edge with regular stitching and trace, leaving a ¼″ gap below the basting stitches.

4. Cut away the red fabric ¼″ beyond the drawn template line on only one side of a triangle at a time and needle-turn appliqué the red fabric along the pencil line to the white fabric. You may want to pin the point of the red triangle that you are appliquéing. As you reach the point, cut away the second side of the triangle and continue appliquéing. Appliqué a V as you move to the next red triangle. When the triangles are appliquéd to the white, release the basting stitches and remove the excess red fabric. Repeat to complete all 8 outer border strips.

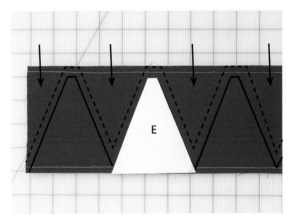

The arrows indicate area of red fabric that will be cut away one side at time, as you needle-turn appliqué the red fabric.

5. Refer to Preparing Appliqué Circles (page 22). Use a card stock template with a 1½″ diameter made from pattern D (pullout page P2) to prepare all the red D circles for appliqué. Position the red D circles evenly on the white fabric between the red triangles and appliqué them in place. Appliqué the remaining 2 red D circles to the 2 border corners with white centers.

6. Use the same technique to prepare 2 white D circles. Appliqué a white D circle to each border corner with a red center.

7. Refer to the quilt assembly diagram to place the red edge of a border strip against a white block background and a white edge of a border strip against a red block background; sew a border strip to one side of each wedge circle block. Trim even with the block edges.

8. Sew a border corner to one end of each remaining border strip. Refer to the quilt assembly diagram to place the corners with red or white centers correctly.

9. Sew the units from Step 8 to the wedge circle blocks, aligning each border corner to the first border strip. Trim the end even with the block.

Quilt Assembly

1. Sew a 1½″ × 23½″ sashing strip to one of the remaining edges of each wedge circle block. Match a red sashing strip with a white block and a white sashing strip with a red block. Add a corresponding 1½″ × 24½″ sashing strip to the remaining edge of each block.

2. Refer to the quilt assembly diagram for the color orientation of the blocks and sashing. Arrange the blocks in 2 rows of 2 blocks as shown, leaving space for the pieced sashing between the 2 rows, with the outer borders toward the outside of the rows and the narrow sashing strips toward the inside. Join the top 2 blocks with a sashing strip in the center, using a sashing strip that is mostly white, with the wide part of the white wedges positioned toward the narrow red sashing strip. Trim evenly with the block edges.

3. Sew the mostly white pieced sashing strips between the blocks to make 2 rows. Trim the sashing even with the blocks.

4. Sew the mostly red pieced sashing strips to either side of the red 3¼″ × 3¼″ square.

5. Sew the pieced sashing from Step 4 between the rows. Trim the sashing even with the blocks.

6. Use a card stock 5½″-diameter template made from pattern B (pullout page P2) to prepare the red B circle for appliqué. Appliqué the circle over the center of the quilt.

Quilt assembly

QUILTING

The Challenge was hand quilted with off-white perle cotton #12. The
majority of the quilting outlines the shapes in the piecing.

WEDGE LOG CABIN

FINISHED QUILT: 70½″ x 70½″ (179 cm x 179 cm) ▪ **FINISHED BLOCK:** 14″ x 14″ (35.5 cm x 35.5 cm)

*I love a wedge, but I also love stripes! Combine the two, and off we go! In **Wedge Log Cabin**, as the name suggests, I used wedges to create slightly wonky Log Cabins row-by-row around the squares. For the border, I have used a clever stripe by Jane Sassaman. This fabric looks like it's pieced already, but it isn't! Then I added a few machine-appliquéd birds around two opposing corners—aren't most cabins surrounded by birds in the branches of trees? The shapes were simple to machine appliqué in place.*

CHOOSING FABRICS

LOG CABIN STRIPES   You can acquire these fabrics in several ways. I used stripes from my stash, so the amounts varied. Suffice it to say that the shortest strips are cut 6¾″ and the largest are 16½″ (20–45 cm). When using scraps, cut from the largest pieces to the smallest for an economical yield. It is possible to use a wide variety of stripes from 2 colors to multiple colors, wide to narrow and everything in between. The fact that they are stripes will do a lot to hold the quilt together.

MATERIALS

Yardage is based on 42"-wide fabric (107 cm), unless otherwise noted.

- **Black homespun / solid cotton:** ½ yard (50 cm) for Log Cabin centers and border appliqués

- **Stripes:** ¼–½ yard (25 cm–50 cm) each of at least 10 different fabrics for Log Cabin wedges

- **Black-and-white prints:** ¼ yard (25 cm) each of at least 3 fabrics for sashing

- **Black-and-white stripe:** ½ yard (50 cm) for inner border and sashing

- **Multicolored print:** ⅝ yard (60 cm) for outer border corners

- **Multicolored stripe:** 1¾ yards (160 cm) for outer border

- **Binding:** ⅝ yard (60 cm)

- **Backing:** 4½ yards (4.1 m)

- **Batting:** 79″ × 79″ (201 cm × 201 cm)

Tools and notions:

- **Stitch stabilizer:** 1½ yards 14″ wide (such as Wash-Away Stitch Stabilizer, by C&T Publishing)

- **Fusible web:** 1¼ yards, 18″ wide (such as Wonder-Under or Vliesofix)

- **Variegated cotton thread:** for appliqué

- *Optional:* 10° wedge ruler, at least 16½″ long

> **note**
>
> *You could use this technique to make skewed Log Cabin blocks from any size wedge. However, if you use a different degree ruler, you will need to cut longer strips.*

All measurements include the seam allowance. Refer to Favorite Techniques (page 17) for information about cutting strips and wedges. Prepare a template from the Wedge Log Cabin *pattern A (pullout page P3), adding the markings to the template. You may use a specialty 10° wedge ruler.*

Black homespun / solid cotton:

- Cut 1 strip 4½″ × width of fabric; subcut 9 squares 4½″ × 4½″ for block centers. Set aside remaining black for border appliqués.

Stripes:

Select 4 fabrics for each block, and use 1 fabric for each round. Cut wedges for 1 block at a time and then make the block before making 8 additional blocks.

For each block:

- Cut 4 wedges, using template A at the 6¾″ mark or 10° wedge ruler (round 1).
- Cut 4 wedges, using template A at the 9¼″ mark or 10° wedge ruler (round 2).
- Cut 4 wedges, using template A at the 12¼″ mark or 10° wedge ruler (round 3).
- Cut 4 wedges, using template A at the 16½″ mark or 10° wedge ruler (round 4).

Black-and-white stripe:

- Cut 5 strips 2½″ × width of fabric for inner borders.

Black-and-white prints (and stripe):

- Cut 6 strips 2½″ × 14½″ for sashing.
- Cut 2 strips 2½″ × 30½″ for sashing.
- Cut 1 strip 2½″ × 32½″ for sashing.

Multicolored print:

- Cut 1 strip 10½″ × width of fabric; subcut 4 squares 10½″ × 10½″ for corner squares.

Multicolored stripe:

- Cut 5 strips 10½ × width of fabric for outer border.

Binding fabric:

- Cut 8 strips 2½″ × width of fabric.

note

Don't sweat the technique about the stripes. They can be cut across the stripe or along the stripe!

SEWING

*All seam allowances are ¼″,
unless otherwise noted.*

Wedge Log Cabin Blocks

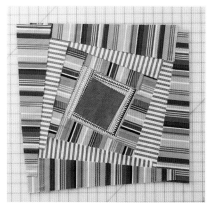

Position the wedges around the block.

1. Starting at the narrow end of the wedge, align a 6¾″ wedge with 1 side of a black 4½″ × 4½″ square. Stitch, then press seams away from the square. Using a straight ruler, trim the excess wide end of the wedge even with the side of the black square. Add the remaining 6¾″ wedges for round 1 in the same fashion, working in a clockwise direction around the block.

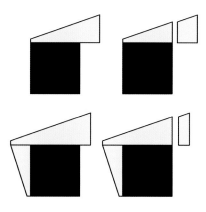

2. Using the same technique as in Step 1, add the 9¼″ wedges for round 2.

3. Continue around the block, adding the 12¾″ wedges and the 16½″ wedges for rounds 3 and 4.

4. Trim the completed block to 14½″ × 14½″, varying the angle of the center square as you go.

5. Repeat Steps 1–4 to make a total of 9 blocks.

Quilt Center

1. On a design wall arrange the 9 squares in 3 rows, leaving space for the sashing strips. Referring to the quilt assembly diagram (next page), position the sashing strips.

2. Sew the blocks and sashing strips together to make the quilt center, following the assembly shown in the quilt assembly diagram.

Inner Border

1. Sew the black-and-white stripe 2½″ strips together end to end. Cut 2 strips 2½″ × 46½″ for side borders and 2 strips 2½″ × 50½″ for top and bottom borders.

2. Find the center of the quilt body and the center of the inner side borders. Matching centers and ends, pin then sew the inner side borders in place.

3. Use the same method to add the top and bottom inner borders.

Appliqués

1. Iron the fusible web to the black homespun / solid cotton. Do not remove the paper backing yet. Along the length of the fusible-backed fabric, freehand cut 4 random branch pieces approximately 25″ long with 1 pointed end. Refer to the quilt photo (next page) to see the branches.

2. Using *Wedge Log Cabin* pattern B (pullout page P3), make a template for the bird. Trace 10 bird shapes onto the paper side of the fusible-backed fabric and cut out along the lines.

Outer Border

1. Sew the multicolored stripe 10½″ strips together end to end. Cut 4 strips 10½″ × 50½″.

2. Place the border strips on a design wall around the quilt center, adding the corner squares. Position the birds and tree branches on the border, letting the branch wander off into the seam allowance. Remove the paper and press in place.

3. Place a sheet of stitch stabilizer on the back of each border, behind the birds and branches. Set your machine to blanket stitch and stitch down the edges of the appliqué. I used a multicolored variegated cotton thread for a bit of colorful detail. Following the manufacturer's instructions, remove the stabilizer before joining the borders to the quilt.

4. Find the center of the body of the quilt and the center of the outer side borders. Pin the centers and ends, then sew into place.

5. Sew a corner square to each end of the top and bottom borders. Pin the centers and ends, and then sew into place.

QUILTING

Wedge Log Cabin was commercially machine quilted by Denise Biviano. A curved-line pattern was used to soften all the straight lines in the block design.

Quilt assembly

RING AROUND

RING AROUND

FINISHED QUILT: 74½″ × 74½″ (189 cm × 189 cm) ▪ **FINISHED BLOCK:** 18″ × 18″ (46 cm × 46 cm)

I work in a fabric shop five to six days a week, which means I am surrounded by fabric. Even after twelve years, I still open a box of fabric as if it is a birthday present and I want to make a quilt! This quilt started with a delivery and quickly got mixed into the pile in my studio. I was toying around with the idea of using the wedge rulers to make circles for wedding ring quilts. I made the quilt top very quickly, but then it took ages before I actually finished it.

CHOOSING FABRICS

BACKGROUNDS *Ring Around* makes use of a nice collection of a favorite graphic, a plaid! Strong plaids, small dotty plaids, and some interesting stripes—all are used as backgrounds in paired sets.

SASHING STRIPS The sashing strips are a wavering stripe that looks different everywhere it is cut, which appeals to me. The eye searches to define what it is seeing. To accentuate the effect, I wove the sashing strips together rather than cutting regular-length strips.

BINDING I love the wild animal prints and thought they added just another quick bit of texture to this quilt.

MATERIALS

Yardage is based on 42"-wide (107 cm) fabric.

- **Plaids and stripes:** ½ yard (50 cm) each of 9 fabrics for backgrounds (Each fabric will be used in 2 quarter-blocks.)
- **Prints for rings:**

  Light print: ⅓ yard (30 cm) for A wedges

  Dark print: ⅜ yard (35 cm) for B wedges

  Assorted prints: ⅛ yard (15 cm) each of 9 different prints for C wedges
- **Wavering stripe:** 1¾ yards (1.6 m) for sashing and inner border
- **Print:** 1⅜ yards (1.3 m) for outer border
- **Binding:** ⅝ yard (60 cm)
- **Backing:** 5 yards (4.6 m)
- **Batting:** 82" × 82" (208 cm × 208 cm)

Tools and notions:

- **Perle cotton #8**
- *Optional:* 18° wedge ruler

CUTTING

All measurements include the seam allowance. Refer to Favorite Techniques (page 17) for information about cutting strips and wedges. Prepare a template from the Ring Around *pattern (pullout page P2), or you may use a specialty 18° wedge ruler. Label the pieces as indicated.*

Each background fabric:

- Cut 1 strip 8½″ × width of fabric; subcut 4 squares 8½″ × 8½″ for ring backgrounds for a total of 36 squares.

Ring fabrics:

Use the Ring Around *template or an 18° wedge ruler marked at the 3¼″ and 5¾″ lines. It is possible to cut several strips at once. Label the wedges as indicated.*

- From the light print, cut 3 strips 2½″ × width of fabric; subcut 40 wedges (A), cutting 10 for each of 4 blocks.
- From the dark print, cut 4 strips 2½″ × width of fabric; subcut 50 wedges (B), cutting 10 for each of 5 blocks.
- From each of the 9 assorted prints, cut 1 strip 2½″ × width of fabric; subcut 10 wedges (C) for a total of 90 wedges.

Cut strips 2½″. Mark your 18° wedge ruler for a 2½″ wedge segment between the 3¼″ and 5¾″ lines on the ruler (or use the *Ring Around* template).

Sashing and inner border fabric:

- Cut 22 strips 2½″ × width of fabric. Join them end to end to make 1 long strip; subcut:

  4 strips 2½″ × 90″ for mitered inner border

  2 strips 2½″ × 28½″

  2 strips 2½″ × 20½″

  12 strips 2½″ × 18½″

  5 strips 2½″ × 10½″

  21 strips 2½″ × 8½″

Print fabric:

- Cut 9 strips 6½″ × width of fabric. Join them end to end to make 1 long strip; subcut 4 strips 6½″ × 90″ for outer border.

Binding fabric:

- Cut 8 strips 2½″ × width of fabric.

SEWING

All seam allowances are ¼", unless otherwise noted.

Rings

1. To make a light ring, use 10 matching A wedges and 10 matching C wedges. For each quarter-ring, join 5 wedges, alternating between A and C wedges. Press all seams open to make appliqué easier. Keep this set together to form a light ring. You'll have:

- 2 quarter-rings with 3 A wedges and 2 C wedges
- 2 quarter-rings with 2 A wedges and 3 C wedges

Join 5 wedges into a quarter-circle.

2. Repeat Step 1 to complete a total of 4 light rings.

3. Repeat Steps 1 and 2, using B wedges and C wedges to make 5 dark rings.

Ring Blocks

1. Refer to the quilt assembly diagram (next page) to place alternating pairs of background squares on a design wall in four-patch groups. Leave room for the sashing pieces.

2. Add sets of quarter-rings on the four-patch groups to make a pleasing arrangement.

3. Working with 1 background group at a time, fold each background square in half on the diagonal and press a crease. Fold the quarter ring sets in half and press a crease at the center. Finger-press a ¼" seam around the inner and outer curves of each ring.

4. Referring to the ring placement diagram, mark 2 adjacent sides of each background square at 5" from the corner and again at 1½" from the opposite end of the side. Using the markings to guide the placement of the ends of the quarter rings, match the center creases in the quarter rings with the center creases in the background squares. Double-check all 4 appliqué placements within a block to be sure they will match up when the rings are joined with the sashing. Pin rings in place and appliqué them to the background squares.

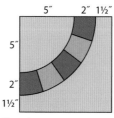

Ring placement

5. Repeat Steps 3 and 4 to appliqué all the rings to the background squares as block groups.

Quilt Body Assembly

1. On a design wall replace the ring sets in 3 rows, dark rings in the corners and center or as you desire. Leave space between each quarter-ring for the sashing strips.

2. Refer to the quilt assembly diagram to place the sashing strips. Start by adding short strips to build units in pairs, then add longer strips to join the pairs and ring sets together as shown.

3. Stitch the sashing strips and quarter-circle squares together, starting in the upper left corner. Join pairs of quarter-circle squares together with a short strip in between. When all the pairs are joined, build in the longer strips until the top is complete.

> **note**
>
> *For a bit of extra interest, I randomly joined the sashing strips across the quilt to break up the grid. If you use a sashing fabric with variations in color, it will look as if the strips are interwoven.*

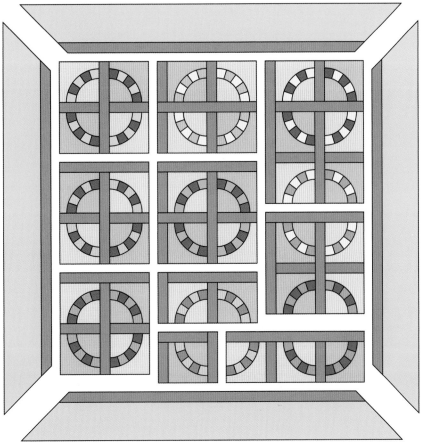

Quilt assembly

Borders

1. Sew a 2½″ × 90″ inside border strip to a 6½″ × 90″ print strip along the long edges to make a border unit. Repeat to make a total of 4 border units. Press the seams open.

2. Measure the body of the quilt. Fold each border unit in half and measure from the center to the point that is half the width and length of the quilt body. Mark this measurement with a pencil on the wrong side of each border unit. Match these points to a point ¼″ from each corner of the quilt body. Match the center of each border unit with the center of the quilt side and pin the border in place.

3. Sew 2 adjacent border units onto the quilt, stopping and backstitching at the points ¼″ from each corner. The excess length of the border units will extend beyond each edge of the quilt. Press the seams toward the borders.

Start stitching ¼″ from edge of quilt top.

4. To create the miter, lay the corner on the ironing board. Working with the quilt right side up, lay 1 border unit on top of the adjacent border unit.

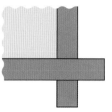
Border unit on top of adjacent unit

5. With right sides up, fold the top border unit under itself so that it meets the edge of the adjacent border unit and forms a 45° angle. Pin the fold in place.

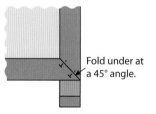
Fold under at a 45° angle.

6. Position a 90° triangle ruler or a square ruler with a 45° line over the corner to check that the corner is flat and square. When everything is in place, press the fold firmly.

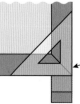
Square corner

7. Remove pins. Fold the center section of the top diagonally from the corner, right sides together, and align the long edges of the border strips. On the wrong side, place pins near the pressed fold in the corner to secure the border strips.

8. Beginning at the inside corner at the border unit seamline, stitch, backstitch, and then stitch along the fold toward the outside point of the border corners, being careful not to allow any stretching to occur. Backstitch at the end. Trim the excess border fabric to a ¼″ seam allowance. Press the seam open.

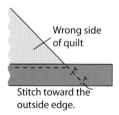
Wrong side of quilt

Stitch toward the outside edge.

QUILTING

Ring Around was machine quilted with stabilizing lines along the sashing strips and double stripes through the border both vertically and horizontally. Then I hand quilted around the rings with orange perle cotton #8.

Just a quick and easy quilt perfect to throw on the lounge!

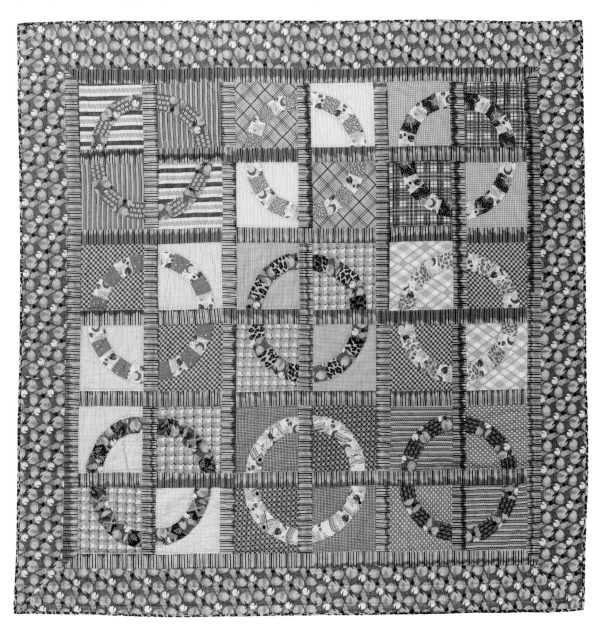

WILD CHILD

FINISHED QUILT: 60½″ × 81½″ (154 cm × 154 cm)

Fabric seems to speak to me. When I get a hankering to work with something, it is like a ghost in my daydreams. Such is the case with the sashing fabric by Jane Sassaman in this quilt. The wide, elongated diamonds cut up into sashing in such a dynamic fashion that I had to use it. The fun here is using these fabrics together to make a story of wild butterflies in the night garden of life!

These blocks are made using 10° wedges and free-form cutting techniques. The instructions will give you the exact sizes to make the top as it is photographed, but it isn't essential to do that. Follow the formula and make adjustments where necessary. I really want this to be a "recipe" for you to create your very own quilt. It was a fun quilt to make—one that grew organically once I got started. Here's how to get wild, child!

CHOOSING FABRICS

BACKGROUND The black-and-white large-scale plant design by Alexander Henry is the perfect partner for dynamic prints and the butterflies that hover above.

WING BLADES I selected pairs that are a combination of Art Gallery prints by Pat Bravo and some funky bits I collected when visiting Britex in San Francisco. The palette is rather unusual, but all the fabrics worked together nicely.

BUTTERFLY BODIES Black homespun for the butterfly bodies seemed the only way to manage holding it all together.

BINDING I used a plaid from one of the wing fabrics. Usually I go for a dark binding, but here I liked the way it combined all the colors of the quilt.

MATERIALS

Yardage is based on 42"-wide (107 cm) fabric, unless otherwise noted.

- **Black-and-white floral:** 4⅛ yards (3.8 m) for background (This amount may vary depending on the size of your blocks.)
- **Color prints:** ⅝ yard (60 cm) each of 12 fabrics to be paired in 6 sets of 2 prints for butterfly wings
- **Black-and-white graphic print:** 1⅞ yards (1.7 m) for sashing and border
- **Black homespun / solid cotton:** ⅜ yard (35 cm) for butterfly bodies
- **Binding:** ⅝ yard (60 cm)
- **Backing:** 5 yards (4.6 m)
- **Batting:** 78″ × 89″ (198 cm × 226 cm)

Tools:

- *Optional:* 10° wedge ruler

CUTTING

All measurements include the seam allowance. Refer to Favorite Techniques (page 17) for information about cutting strips and wedges. Prepare the Wild Child *patterns A and B (pullout page P3), or you may use commercial templates or specialty rulers.*

Color prints:

Use template A or a 10° wedge ruler marked at 22″.

For each set of butterfly wings, use 2 fabrics: fabric A and fabric B. Cut 6 sets of wings. Keep them together as sets.

- Cut 8–10 wedges from fabric A, using template A.
- Cut 6–8 wedges from fabric B, using template A.

Background fabric:

Don't cut all of these squares at once. Cut only 2 squares and make 1 block. Depending on how large you want to cut your final blocks, you may not need to use 21″ × 21″ background squares for every block. You can decide to use smaller squares for your own plan.

- Cut 6 strips 21″ × width of fabric; subcut 12 squares 21″ × 21″.

Sashing fabric:

Don't cut the sashing until you have completed and trimmed the blocks. Refer to the quilt assembly diagram (page 87) for my layout. These are the measurements for my quilt. If you trim your blocks differently, measure your blocks for your exact dimensions and adjust the sizes of these sashing pieces to your unique blocks.

- Cut 9 strips 6½″ × width of fabric. From the strips, subcut:
  2 strips 6½″ × 34½″
  2 strips 6½″ × 29½″
  1 strip 6½″ × 27½″
  2 strips 6½″ × 26½″
  2 strips 6½″ × 22½″
  1 strip 6½″ × 20½″
  2 strips 6½″ × 13½″

Binding fabric:

- Cut 8 strips 2½″ × width of fabric.

SEWING

All seam allowances are ¼", unless otherwise noted.

Wing Wedges

Using 1 set of wing wedges, join the wedges along the long edges, narrow ends together, alternating between fabric A and fabric B. For each butterfly, make 2 identical wings, each with 7–9 wedges, to form a pair of wings. Make 6 pairs of wings.

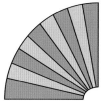

Alternate A and B fabric wedges to form wing.

Butterfly Bodies

1. Refer to Preparing Appliqué Shapes (page 22). Use template B and a chalk pencil to trace 6 butterfly bodies onto the black fabric. Cut out the B pieces.

2. Finger-press the seam allowance to the back of all 6 B pieces. Set aside until the rest of the block is assembled.

Block Assembly

Here's the tricky part (it is hard only because the science isn't exact … however, it is easy when you get the hang of it!). Here's how to sew the wings to the background squares. Using the 21" × 21" background squares will allow you to cut the blocks the sizes that I used, but you may want to vary the block sizes in your quilt.

1. Place a 21" × 21" background square right side up on a cutting mat. Arrange a pair of wings, also right side up, on top of the background, overlapping 2 adjacent edges of the square. Position the wings so that the inner tips of both just meet in the center. The open area between the wings will be covered by the butterfly body. It is a good idea to use template B to check that it will be covered by the butterfly body. Mark the inner point where the 2 wings meet on the square.

Position wings on top of background piece. Mark the inner point.

2. Align a ruler with the edge of a wing and make a cut through the background fabric as shown.

Align a ruler with the edge of a wing and cut through the background.

3. Remove the lower wing. Gently flip the upper wing on top of the background fabric right sides together as shown, matching the point you marked on the background in Step 1 with the inner point of the wing. Pin together, then join with a ¼″ seam allowance. Press flat with the seam allowance toward the wing.

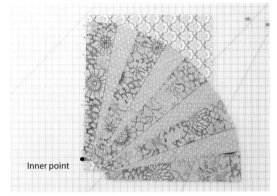

Flip, pin, sew, and press.

4. Again smooth out the unit from Step 3 on the cutting surface and replace the lower wing on the background square. Make a cut along the top edge of the lower wing as shown. Repeat the flipping, pinning, stitching, and pressing as before.

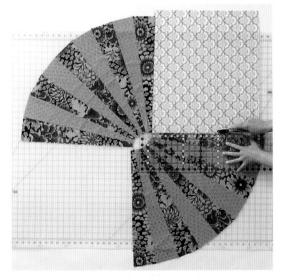

Position ruler over the top edge of the second wing.

5. Repeat Steps 1–4, using another 21″ × 21″ background square as shown. Cut, flip, pin, stitch, and press. The block should lie flat when it is pressed.

Position the unit from Step 4 on top of another background square for the lower section of the block.

6. You can use graph paper to plan out the block sizes for your own design, using this "block recipe" for sewing your blocks. You may want to consider using smaller background squares to construct the remaining 5 blocks. If you are following my quilt construction, repeat Steps 1–5 to complete a total of 6 blocks.

> **note**
>
> *Your wings will be curved around the outer edges. If you wish, you can fold back the edges to get an idea of how big you want them to be before cutting the block. Consider if you want the butterfly centered in the block or offset.*

7. Your butterfly placements do not have to match mine. Arrange the wings however you like and trim the blocks to fit your own plan if you like, but below are the measurements I used to trim my blocks. Refer to the quilt assembly diagram so you know the block placement in the quilt. Using a square ruler is a big help here to get the corners square as you trim.

- **Block 1:** 20½″ × 22½″
- **Block 2:** 25½″ × 26½″
- **Block 3:** 20½″ × 16½″
- **Block 4:** 22½″ × 29½″
- **Block 5:** 22½″ × 13½″
- **Block 6:** 28½″ × 27½″

8. Appliqué a butterfly body to the space between the wings.

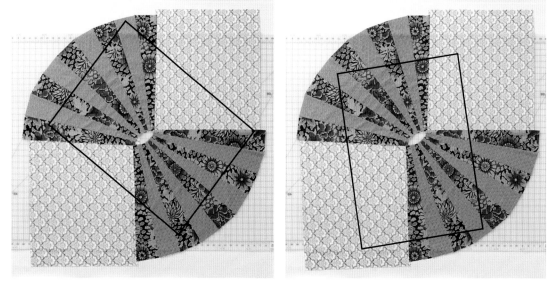

Cut the various block sizes from the large units, shifting the butterfly angles.

Wild Child, 62″ × 88″
made and quilted by Helena Fooij

Helena used the *Wild Child* pattern and the Tula Pink Elizabeth range to create her own version. The sashing varies throughout the quilt, and in the outer border some of the wedges extend out, creating an interesting line pattern. Helena did the machine quilting herself and did a beautiful job!

Quilt Assembly

1. If you followed my measurements, position the blocks and sashing pieces according to the quilt assembly diagram on a design wall. If you designed your own layout, follow your graph paper design.

2. Sew the sashing strips to the blocks as shown in the quilt assembly diagram.

3. Sew the blocks into columns.

4. Matching the centers and ends together, pin the 2 columns and then sew together.

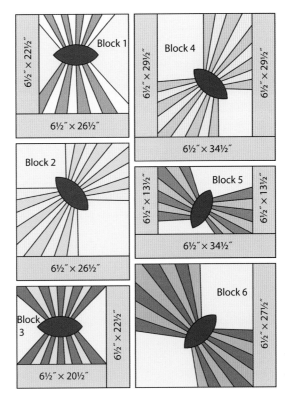

Quilt assembly

QUILTING

When the top is complete, layer and baste. I stabilized the sashing strips and then did allover quilting in the blocks. You may enjoy doing the same!

AT THE MACHINE

My most natural state of quilting is acting on impulse. Generally, the process starts with a fabric that sparks my imagination. It feels as though it speaks to me—"cut me this way," "feature this design," "find this color"—and then I am off! The intuitive reactions are strong and I often find myself on the road to somewhere very quickly. For these kinds of moments, working on the machine is the only way forward as results need to be immediate.

INTO THE WOODS

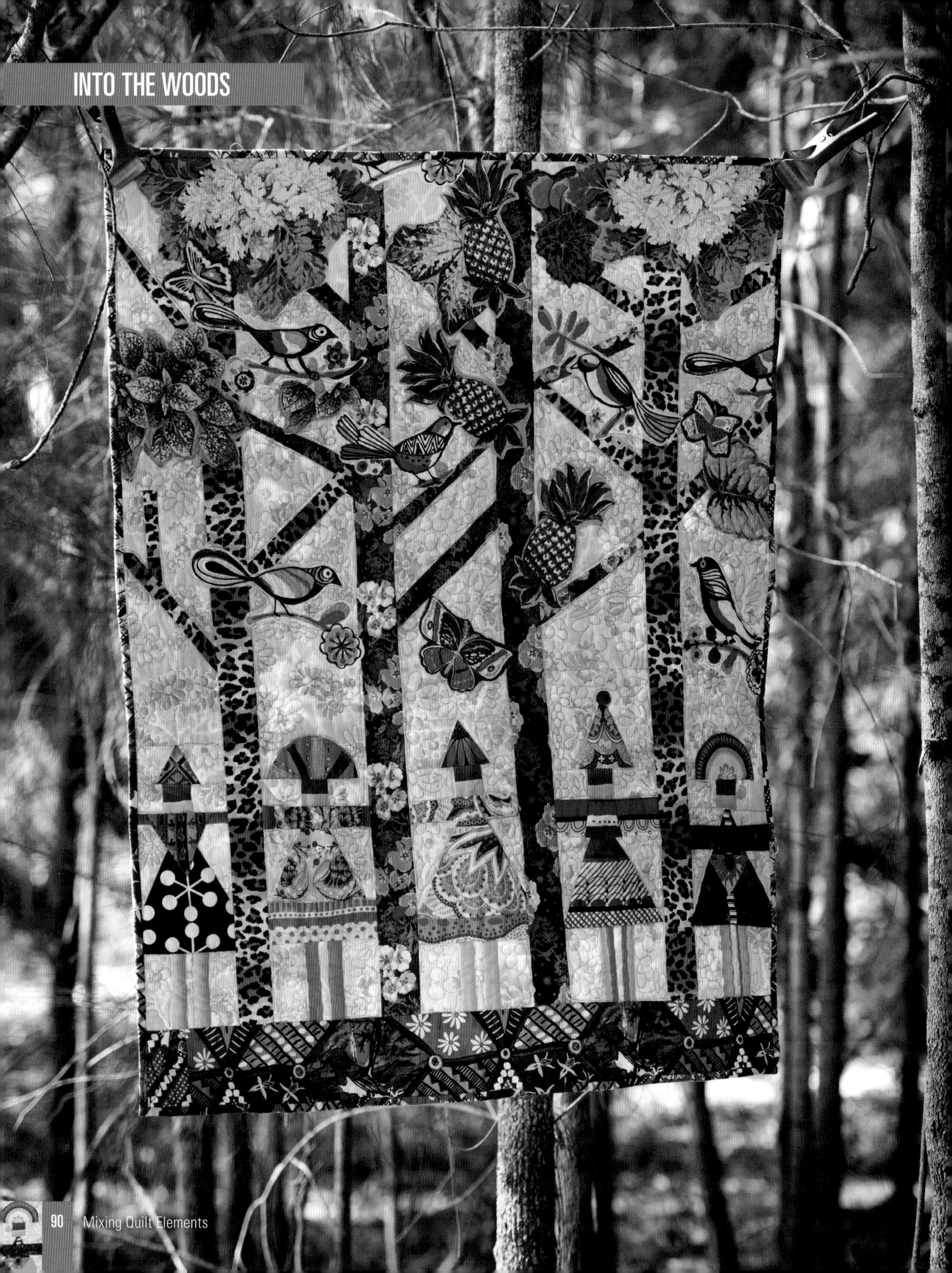

INTO THE WOODS

FINISHED QUILT: 36″ x 44½″ (91 cm x 113 cm)

As a girl I liked nothing better than to disappear into the fantasy world I found as I wandered in the woods under the protective covering of the leafy branches. On the constant lookout for furry creatures and often singing, I would wander for hours, sometimes wishing to be lost but never finding myself so.

The fun of this quilt is the multilayered technique of wonky cuts made famous by Gwen Marston and Freddy Moran in **Collaborative Quilting** as well as a quilt-as-you-go method, raw-edge appliqué, and, well, just a bit of imagination. Funky hats and lively outfits are the required dress code for the day for this trip into the woods.

CHOOSING FABRICS

DOLLS Here is a chance to use all the special scraps of your favorite fabrics to dress the dolls. Use detail or hardly any to make their clothes and hats. The girl figures are in colorful dresses with funky hats. Each one is an individual character, perhaps even from different countries. They stand linked in spirit alone in the woods under the leafy treetops filled with birds and flowers.

TREES If it reminds you of the texture of bark, you can use it. I used florals and animal prints, but plaids, checks, polka dots— anything will do it if makes you think of a tree trunk.

LEAVES These are raw-edge appliquéd onto the finished top with the butterfly and bird motifs. Search your stash for special treats that take the mind on a path of discovery and fun!

BASE The ground is an aboriginal print, but the effect is that of fallen leaves on the forest floor. Use your imagination. That is what life is all about!

The technique is also fun for this quilt. First, make all the young ladies; then build the strips working from left to right so that it can be machine quilted as-you-go.

MATERIALS

Yardage is based on 42"-wide (107 cm) fabric.

Forest:

- **Pale green floral:** 1¾ yards (1.6 m) for background
- **Tree trunk fabrics:** ¼ yard (25 cm) each of 4 different fabrics
- **Leafy fabric:** ½ yard (50 cm)

Motifs to place in trees:

- **Bird print fabric:** ½ yard (50 cm)
- **Earth fabric:** ¼ yard (25 cm) for forest floor
- **Miscellaneous scraps** with pineapples, flowers, butterflies, or other shapes

Dolls:

- **Prints:** approximately 6″ × 6″ (15 cm × 15 cm) scraps of 5 different fabrics for dresses
- **Scraps:** for hats
- **Skin tones:** ¼ yard (25 cm)

Finishing:

- **Binding:** ½ yard (50 cm)
- **Backing:** 1½ yards (1.2 m)
- **Fusible batting:** 42″ × 52″ (107 cm × 132 cm)

- -

CUTTING

See sewing directions for additional cutting information.

Binding fabric:

- Cut 5 strips 2½″ × width of fabric.

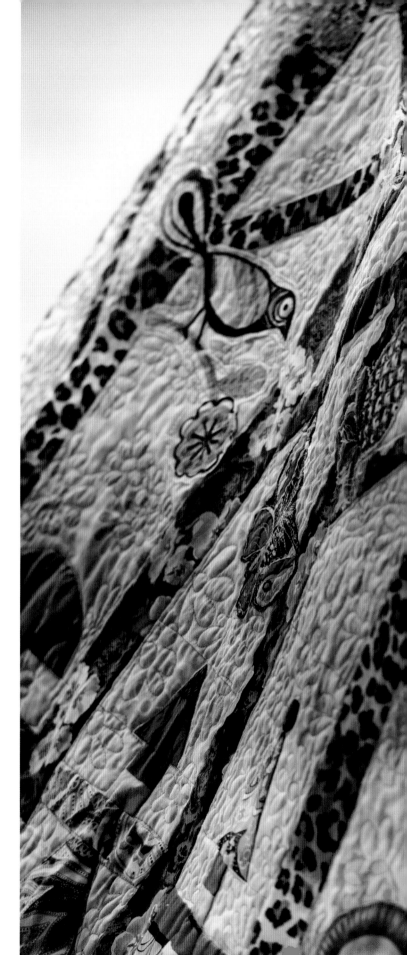

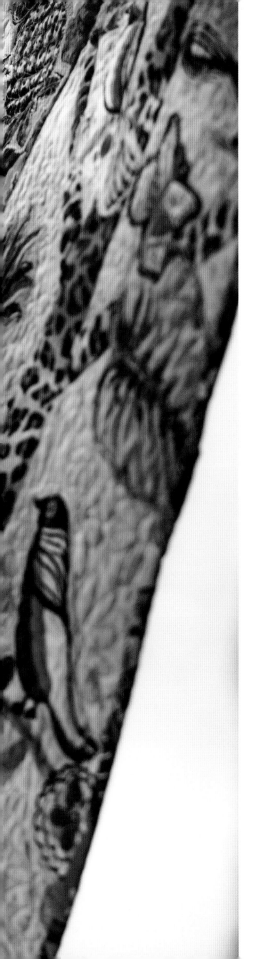

SEWING

All seam allowances are ¼", unless otherwise noted.

Making Dolls

These dolls are improvised using a few quick-cut methods. If you have never done this before, it is a good idea to have a practice. Once you get the hang of it, you'll love it. The dolls are a great way to use up your special scraps and some of the ribbons and buttons you may have collected as well.

The instructions give measurements for making the dolls, though you can use these measurements as guidelines to create your own versions of the dolls. Look ahead to what comes next. Consider how you are most comfortable making the dolls. If you like appliqué, you can make them using that skill. If you like tall, skinny dolls, elongate the instructions and so on. You could make one doll at a time to get the hang of it and then proceed with more dolls.

LEGS

These directions are for making all 5 sets of legs at once, or make a set at a time so you can have a variety of legs.

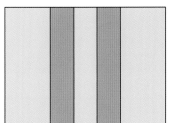

Doll legs assembly

Skin fabric:

- Cut 2 rectangles 1½" × 25".

Background fabric:

- Cut 1 rectangle 1½" × 25".
- Cut 2 rectangles 2½" × 25".

1. Sew the leg fabrics together in this order:

- 2½" background strip
- 1½" leg strip
- 1½" background strip
- 1½" leg strip
- 2½" background strip

2. Cut the pieced strip into 5 equal parts to make a set of legs for each doll. This gives you sections 5" high. You can vary the width and length of the legs by making each strip section individually.

SKIRT

Make the skirts one at a time. You can vary the skirts to be wider and longer.

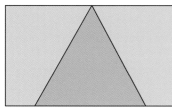
Doll skirt assembly

Background fabric:

- Cut 2 rectangles 6½″ × 4½″ for each skirt.

Dress fabric:

- Cut a triangle 4½″ tall, using a 60° ruler or freehand cutting at a random angle.

1. Place a background rectangle right side up on a flat cutting surface. Place the triangle, also right side up, on top of the rectangle, aligning the center of the triangle with the right edge of the background rectangle. Use a rotary cutter and ruler to cut the background rectangle flush with the edge of the triangle. Discard the cut background piece under the triangle.

Align center of triangle on top of right edge of rectangle.

2. Gently flip the background rectangle over the dress fabric so they are right sides together, matching the cut edges. Pin, then join with a ¼″ seam. Press.

3. Place the other background rectangle right side up on the cutting surface. Place the unit from Step 2, also right side up on top of the rectangle, aligning the center of the triangle with the right edge of the background rectangle. Use a rotary cutter and ruler to make a cut in the background fabric flush with the edge of the triangle. Discard the cut rectangle piece under the triangle.

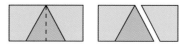

4. Repeat Step 2.

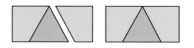

5. Repeat Steps 1–4 to make 5 skirt units. You can vary the skirts by varying the height of the triangle in each skirt and cutting the background rectangles 6½″ × the height of each triangle.

ARMS

Make the arm units one at a time.

Doll arms assembly

These measurements can vary between dolls to make the sleeves longer or shorter.

Dress fabric or complementary scrap:

- Cut 1 rectangle 1½″ × 4½″.

Skin fabric:

- Cut 2 rectangles 1½″ × 2″.

1. Join a skin rectangle to each end of the dress fabric rectangle.

2. Make a total of 5 arm sections, varying the length of the dress and skin pieces.

3. Trim each arm section to 6″ long with equal lengths for each arm.

HEAD

Make the head units one at a time.

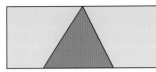

Doll head assembly

Skin fabric:

- Cut 5 squares 1½″ × 1½″.

Background fabric:

- Cut 10 rectangles 1½″ × 3″.

1. Join a background rectangle to each side of a doll head.

2. Make 5. For variety, look at the quilt photo (page 99) to see that you could piece the square so the top half of the head has "hair."

HATS

Make the hats one at a time.

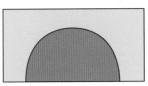

Small hat assembly

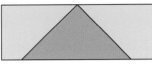

Curved assembly

Big hat assembly

I used 3 shapes—a half-circle, a wide triangle, and a sharp triangle. You can use any shape you like or let the fabric dictate with a fussy-cut motif.

Hat fabrics:

- Freehand-cut triangles or half-circles from print fabric, letting the print help you decide the shape.

Background fabrics:

- Cut 2 rectangles 3½″ × ½″ taller than the triangle for each triangle hat.
- Cut 1 rectangle 6″ × ¾″ taller than the half-circle for each moon hat.

1. Refer to the sewing directions for the Skirt (previous page) to join the triangle hat sections.

2. Appliqué a half-circle piece to a background rectangle for the curved hat.

DOLL ASSEMBLY

1. For each doll, arrange the pieced doll sections, centering each one. Join together with a ¼″ seam. Press.

2. Trim all 5 doll sections to a consistent width. The sections may vary in height because of the variety of hats used in each doll. I trimmed my doll sections to a consistent 6″ width.

Join the pieced doll sections. Trim to equal width.

Branches

Each of 4 tree fabrics:

- Cut 1 strip 2½" × width of fabric for tree trunks.
- Cut 1 strip 1½" × width of fabric for branches.
- Cut 1 strip 1" × width of fabric for branches.

Background fabric:

- Cut 5 strips 7" × 25".

1. Place a background 7" × 25" strip right side up on a cutting surface. Make a random diagonal cut through the background fabric.

2. Sew a branch strip (1" or 1½" wide) to one side of the cut. Press, then join the other side of the cut background to the branch. Trim branch ends even with the background. Refer to the quilt photo to see the branches. When selecting the branch fabric for the background piece, think about what tree trunk fabric will be next in your layout since you may want to have some branches of the same tree trunk fabric in the adjacent background pieces.

You have to think ahead a bit!

3. Add 1 or 2 more branches, using the same process. Make branches from the 1" and 1½" strips for variety. The width of the background will change as you add branches. Do not join the tree trunk to this branch section yet, but in the photo you can see how the tree trunk will will look with the branches. Trim the background/branch unit to the same width as a doll section. I trimmed mine to 6" wide.

4. Join the doll section to the bottom end of the branch background to make a long column.

5. Repeat Steps 1–4 with the remaining doll units and branch background strips.

6. When all 5 columns are finished, measure the shortest column and trim the other 4 columns to match, trimming off the excess at the top of the columns. I trimmed my columns to 40" long. Do not join the columns together yet. You can add more branches in the quilt-as-you-go steps.

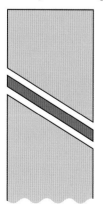

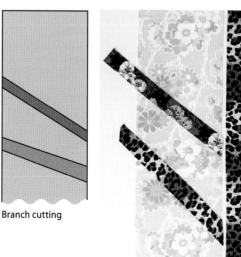

Branch cutting

With the tree trunk fabric in position next to the background, you can see how the branch fabric strips through the background make great branches, but do not join the tree trunk to the branch section now!

Quilt-As-You-Go Assembly

1. Fuse the wrong side of the backing 42″ × 52″ fabric to one side of the fusible batting, following the manufacturer's instructions. If you do not have this product available, you can use fusible interfacing to fuse the batting and fabric together.

2. Place the backing fabric facedown on an ironing surface with the batting on top. Arrange the first doll column 2″ from the left edge and the top of the doll column 3″ from the top of the batting. Press to fuse, being careful to protect your iron from the glue.

3. To machine quilt, drop the feed dogs and use a darning or free-motion foot on your machine. Work from the center top of the quilt to the outside. Be sure to secure the threads with a knot stitch and leave an end to bury on top, or start with very small stitches (1.3–1.5) and increase the length (2.75–3.0) after 5 or 6 stitches.

4. Machine quilt through all 3 layers of the doll column, using a random squiggle or leaf pattern. I like to look for quilt patterns within the pattern of the fabric.

tip

Start by stabilizing the section—stitching-in-the-ditch around the tree branches, across the skirt, and down the legs. (I didn't do this on my quilt, but I have learned a few tricks and would advise this now!) Use your preferred filler stitch, which might be a pebble stitch, leafy pattern, or just parallel lines. Or look for quilt patterns within the pattern of the fabric.

5. From the tree fabric coordinating the branches in the first section, trim a 2½″-wide tree trunk strip to the length of your quilted doll strip and align it, right sides together, along the edge of the pieced section. Stitch a ¼″ seam through all the layers. Flip and press flat. Quilt a bark design onto the tree strip.

6. Repeat this process, aligning the next doll column with the quilted section, stitching a ¼″ seam, and flipping the column to continue quilting. Add the next tree trunks and doll columns to the quilt. You can make your quilt the project size or any size you wish.

7. When all the tree and doll columns are pieced together, you can add more branches, and you'll be ready to decorate the treetops. This is a great way to practice your machine quilting while finishing the quilt as you go!

Treetops and Ground

Leafy fabric:

■ Fussy cut leaves for trees.

Bird print fabric:

■ Fussy cut birds for treetops.

Miscellaneous scraps:

■ Fussy cut pineapples, butterflies, or other shapes.

Earth fabric:

■ Cut 1 strip 5½″ × width of fabric.

1. Lay the leaves, birds, and motifs out over the treetops and pin in place with flat-head pins. These pins secure the fussy-cut fabrics in place and are easy to slide out when quilting.

2. Follow the designs in the fabrics to machine quilt the raw-edge pieces in place.

3. Measure across your quilt top and trim the 5½″-wide earth strip to that length. Place the earth strip right sides together and even with the quilt bottom. Join the ground fabric to the bottom edge of the quilted piece, flip down, and machine quilt in place.

4. When all the quilting is finished, square up your quilt and bind.

Voilà: You are done!

COLOR WORKS

FINISHED QUILT: 65½″ × 84″ (166 cm × 216 cm) ▪ FINISHED BLOCK: 16½″ × 16½″ (42 cm × 42 cm)

Color makes us happy. Contemporary fabrics today are full of exciting color. To make it work, balance bright, saturated colors with earthy, more tonal fabrics. **Color Works** *is an opportunity to combine all those vivacious, big-print fabrics in your stash with shot cotton stripes as you might see them in a natural surround. Light and shade add interest, so remember that every garden has brown!*

Here is an exercise using vibrant polychromatic prints that can be added to your stash of batiks or hand-dyed fabrics! The thing that brings them together is that they are beautiful, bombastic hits of print and color balanced by the contrast of the shadowy, earthy colors as if we are seeing them in the real world.

The border of this quilt is a thrifty use of the leftovers from cutting the quilt.

CHOOSING FABRICS

BLOCKS Select a variety of polychromatic prints and mix them with monochromatic hand dyes or batiks. The ones I used are by Marcia Derse.

SASHING The sashing strips are shot cotton stripes by Kaffe Fassett, which have lots of color shot through with the same earthy look to perfectly complement the loud feature prints.

BORDER The border is simply a combination of the scraps, which further consolidate the palette with additional pattern.

MATERIALS

Yardage is based on 42"-wide (107 cm) fabric.

- **Feature prints:** ⅞ yard (80 cm) each of 12 fabrics for large X, cornerstones, and outer border
- **Stripes:** ¼ yard (25 cm) each of 12 fabrics for thin crosses, sashings, and inner border
- **Monochromatic prints, hand dyes, or batiks:** ½ yard (50 cm) each of 12 fabrics for block background triangles and border

- **Binding:** ⅝ yard (60 cm)
- **Backing:** 5¼ yards (4.8 m)
- **Batting:** 74″ × 92″ (188 cm × 234 cm)

Tools:

- *Optional:* 45°/90° triangle ruler

CUTTING

All measurements include the seam allowance. Refer to Favorite Techniques (page 17) for information about cutting strips.

Each of 12 feature prints:

- Cut 2 strips 5½″ × width of the fabric; subcut 1 strip 5½″ × 25″ and 2 strips 5½″ × 10½″.
- Cut 1 square 8¾″ × 8¾″; subcut diagonally twice to yield 4 quarter-square triangles (48 total for all 12 prints). You will need 36 of these for outer border. Save the rest for another project.
- Cut 2 squares 2½″ × 2½″ for sashing cornerstones. You will have extra cornerstones.

Each of 2 feature prints:

- Cut 1 square 4½″ × 4½″; subcut diagonally once to yield 2 triangles each (4 total) for ends of side borders.

Each of 12 stripe fabrics:

- Cut 1 strip 2½″ × width of fabric from each; subcut 1 strip 2½″ × 22″ for pieced blocks and 1 strip 2½″ × 17″ for sashing.
- Cut 1 strip 2½″ × width of fabric; subcut 2 strips 2½″ × 17″ for sashing. You will have extra sashing pieces.

Each of 12 monochromatic prints, hand dyes, or batiks:

- Cut 2 strips 5½″ × width of fabric from each; subcut 1 strip 5½″ × 22″ for background of each block (total of 24 strips).

Binding fabric:

- Cut 8 strips 2½″ × width of fabric.

SEWING

All seam allowances are ¼", unless otherwise noted.

Blocks

1. Join a matching monochromatic print 5½" × 22" strip to each side of a striped 2½" × 22" strip. Then cut the strip set into 4 rectangles 5½" × 12½".

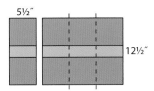

Subcut the strip set into 4 rectangles.

2. Prepare a template from the *Color Works* pattern (pullout page P2). Using the template or a quarter-square triangle ruler, cut a large triangle from each pieced rectangle as shown. The 96 smaller sections you cut away will be used in the border later, so save them.

Use the template to cut the large triangle, saving smaller sections.

3. Sew a pieced triangle unit from Step 2 to each side of a 5½" × 10½" feature strip as shown. Lightly press. Repeat with the other 2 matching triangle units and 10½" feature strip.

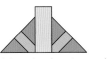

Join a triangle unit to each side of a 10½" feature strip.

4. Marking the centers of each triangle and the center of the matching 5½" × 25" feature strip, pin the centers together and sew a unit from Step 3 to each side of the strip.

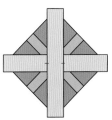

Sew the unit from Step 3 to each side of the 25" feature strip.

5. To complete the block, trim as needed to square up the block to 17" × 17". Use a ruler to trim the corners of the block to neat 90° angles as shown.

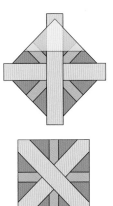

Square up the corners of the block.

6. Repeat Steps 1–5 to make 11 more blocks.

Quilt Body Assembly

1. Refer to the quilt assembly diagram to arrange the blocks in 4 rows of 3 blocks each.

2. Position the striped sashing strips vertically between the blocks and at the left and right end of each row. Join each row together.

3. Position the sashing strips and cornerstones in place to form the sashing strip rows. Join together.

4. Matching the seams, join the sashing strips and block rows to complete the quilt body.

Quilt assembly

Borders

1. Refer to the quilt assembly diagram to arrange the outside border rows. Begin each border row with a feature half-square triangle that was cut from the 4½″ × 4½″ square and add the 36 feature quarter-square triangles that were cut from the 8¾″ squares around the outside of the quilt, with the long side of the triangle next to the quilt body.

2. Trim 4½″ half-square triangles from the leftover sections as shown. You should have 96 half-square triangles.

3. Sew the 96 half-square triangles from Step 2 together in pairs.

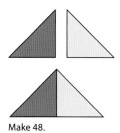

Make 48.

4. Arrange the units from Step 3 between the feature triangles to fill in the border with the long edge of each pair toward the outside. Stand back and make sure you are happy with how the colors and tones are spread around the border. You will have extras to save for another project.

5. Sew the triangles together for the top and bottom borders. Sew the border strips to the top and bottom of the quilt, matching the border centers with the quilt center and pinning the ends. Trim the strips even with the quilt as needed.

6. Sew the triangles together for the side borders, using a half-square triangle cut from a feature print 7″ × 7″ square on one end of a border if you need more length for the border sections.

7. Sew the side borders to the quilt, matching the border centers to the quilt center and pinning the ends. Trim the borders even with the top and bottom borders.

That's it—your quilt top is complete.

QUILTING

I quilted *Color Works* with perle cotton #8 in a variety of colors. Generally, with a quilt that has a lot of color and print fabric, I follow the setting lines of the blocks. This way the lines and shapes are accented, the quilt is stabilized, and the fabrics are left to be the feature.

BALLROOM DANCING

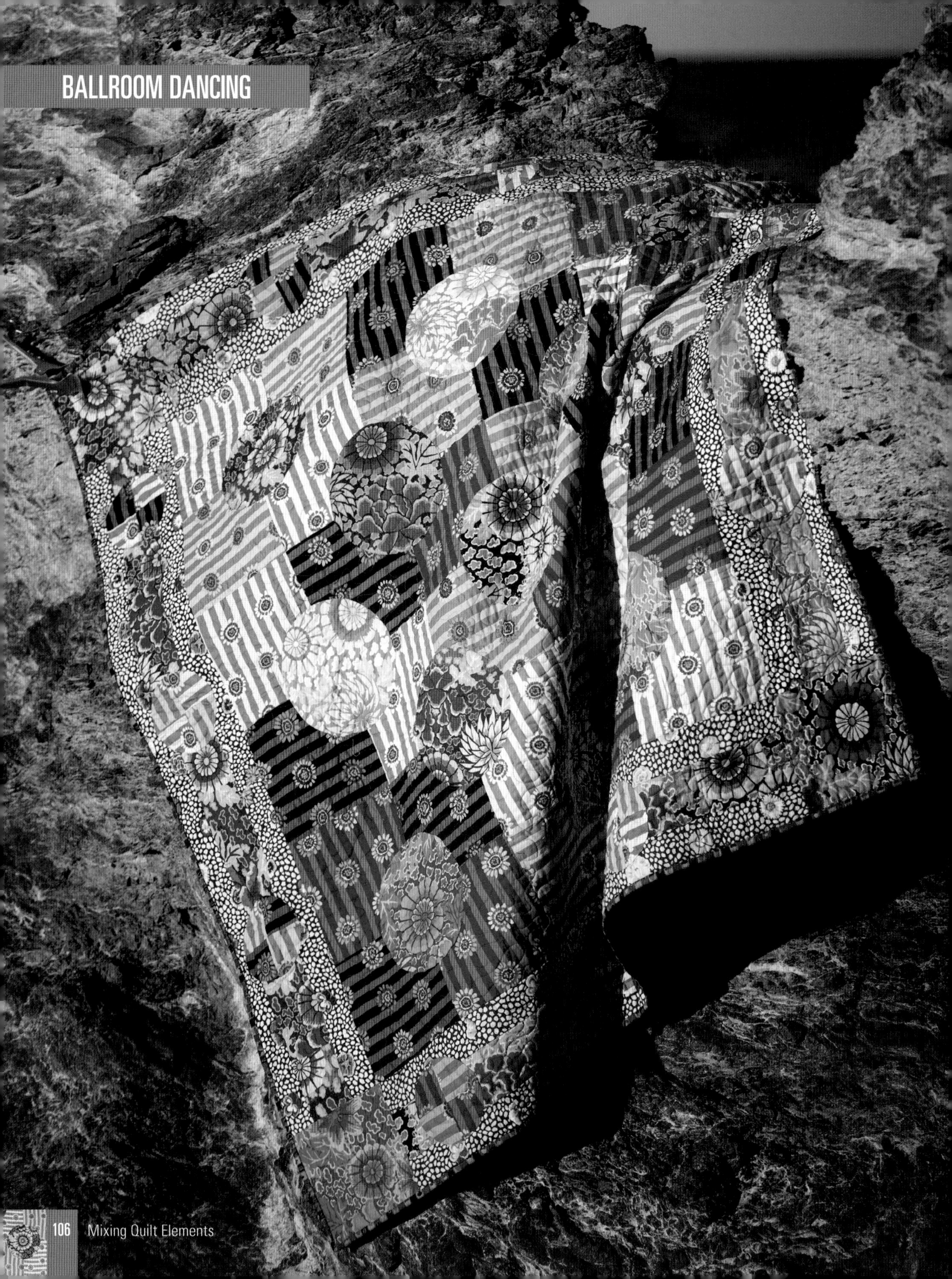

BALLROOM DANCING

FINISHED QUILT: 59½" x 59½" (151 cm x 151 cm) ▪ **FINISHED BLOCK:** 15" x 15" (38 cm x 38 cm)

Mixing elements is a combination of design and technique considerations. For example, a nice, round line will produce softened shapes and add impact to a quilt made of straight lines. The mixture adds contrast in pattern effectively. Curved lines work nicely to complement floral fabrics, whereas stripes strongly reinforce linear patterned fabrics, adding visual excitement.

Sewn-in circles look harder to make than they are. I admit that making them is a skill I avoided for many years. Just remember the background circle is smaller than the inset circle, and you'll be fine! The main thing is that, when looking at a quilt, it is up to you to decide which method of construction you prefer! Consider trying this quilt with set-in circles by following the instructions, or you may prefer to appliqué the circles with a machine stitch like a buttonhole or zigzag. Or, you could choose to needle-turn appliqué the circle in place. In all cases, if you have a favorite technique, feel free to use it!

CHOOSING FABRICS

I love the way the florals are showcased in the circles set on the striking stripe background. There is something undeniably exciting about stripe fabrics. They create a dynamic movement throughout a quilt that attracts and holds the eye.

The fabrics used here are by Kaffe Fassett. Each season he and his team of designers deliver a dependable collection of large-scale, colorful fabrics with a mixture of graphic prints. If the fabrics in the model are no longer available, take a quick look through a current collection to find suitable substitutes of equal value and interest.

STRIPES I used several colors of the same stripe, but a combination of varied stripes would also work.

BORDERS I used two colors of one print, with the remaining bits of the floral prints to make the border. The pieced circles are cut from the background behind the large circle appliqués in the blocks.

MATERIALS

Yardage is based on 42"-wide (107 cm) fabric.

- **Assorted florals:** ¾ yard (70 cm) each of 5 colors—red, green, brown, blue, and gray—for circles and middle border strips
- **Stripes:**

  ¾ yard (70 cm) each of 4 colors—red, green, brown, and gray

  ½ yard (50 cm) of blue for first and third border strips

- **Spotted print/floral:** ½ yard (50 cm) each of 2 colorways for the outer border strips (I used a guinea floral in a green colorway and a gray colorway.)
- **Binding:** ½ yard (50 cm)
- **Backing:** 3⅞ yards (3.4 m)
- **Batting:** 68" × 68" (173 cm × 173 cm)

Tools:

- *Optional:* 5½", 7½", and 8½" circle templates

CUTTING

All measurements include the seam allowance. Refer to Favorite Techniques (page 17) for information about cutting strips and appliqué. Prepare a template from the Ballroom Dancing *pattern A (pullout page P1), adding the markings.*

Florals:

- Cut 3 circles 8½" from each of 5 florals, using template A for a total of 15 circles. You will have 2 extra circles.
- Cut 1 square 7½" × 7½" from each of only 4 florals for border corners.
- Cut 2 strips 3½" × width of fabric from each of only 4 florals. Join end to end, then subcut a strip 3½" × 45½" for center of border section.

Stripes:

From the blue stripe:
- Cut 1 strip 8" × width of fabric; subcut 4 squares 8" × 8".

From the gray stripe:
- Cut 2 strips 8" × width of fabric; subcut 10 squares 8" × 8".

From the green stripe:
- Cut 2 strips 8" × width of fabric; subcut 6 squares 8" × 8".

From each of the red and brown stripes:
- Cut 2 strips 8" × width of fabric; subcut 8 squares 8" × 8".

Each of 2 spotted florals:

- Cut 5 strips 2½" × the width of fabric. Join end to end to make a long strip and subcut 4 strips 2½" × 45½".

Binding fabric:

- Cut 7 strips 2½" × width of fabric.

SEWING

All seam allowances are ¼″, unless otherwise noted.

Block Assembly

Choose 2 striped 8″ × 8″ squares and 2 contrasting striped
8″ × 8″ squares for each block. Arrange the squares
in a 4-block formation, alternating the direction of
the stripes. Join together in pairs, then sew the pairs
together to complete a Four-Patch block. Make 9.

Arrows show
direction of stripes.

Adding the Circles

The floral A circles are sewn into the blocks in the quilt center of
this project. However, if you prefer to appliqué the blocks, refer to
the note.

> **note**
>
> *If you would rather appliqué the floral circles over the block
> intersections, don't cut out a circle from every intersection. Instead,
> make an 8˝ circle template from card stock and use it to prepare all the
> floral A circles for appliqué, adding your preferred seam allowance
> for applique. Refer to Preparing Appliqué Circles (page 22). Stitch
> the prepared circles to the block intersections, using your favorite
> appliqué method. When you finish the appliqué, carefully cut out the
> backgrounds behind the appliqué circles so you can use them for the
> pieced border circles.*

1. To sew the circles into the blocks, first make a card stock
template B with the template marks, using *Color Works* pattern B.
Position the template on the cross seams of a Four-Patch block,
centering the template over the intersection of the block. Trace and
cut out the circle neatly, saving this cutaway circle for the border.
Repeat on all 9 blocks. Do not appliqué the circles yet.

2. Refer to the quilt assembly diagram (page 110). On a design wall
position the Four-Patch blocks (with the holes) in 3 rows, 3 blocks
each, so that the direction of the stripes alternates in every other
square. When you have the block colors arranged to your liking, make
a pleasing arrangement with the floral A circles over the block holes.
Take a photo of your design wall so you know the circle placement.

3. To sew the circle into a block, begin by pressing the floral A circle in half and then in half again to crease 90° markings on the circle. Position the circle right side up. Lay the block right side up on top of the circle, aligning the seamlines with the creases of the circle. Turn under the right side of the outer circle (the curved edge of the block) to meet the right side of the floral circle, aligning the raw edges and matching the seamlines to the creases with right sides together. Pinning from the wrong side of the block, use a lot of pins to ease the curve of the block onto the curve of the floral circle. Continue pinning around the circle.

Match seamlines of block with creases of circle.

4. Position the pinned unit at the sewing machine with the floral circle on the bottom against the feed dogs. Sew slowly, being sure to maintain an accurate ¼″ seam allowance around the circle. After the circle is sewn, fix any tucks or gathers in the seam if needed. Press the block flat.

5. Repeat Steps 3 and 4 to sew a floral A circle in the center of each Four-Patch block to make a total of 9 blocks. Return the blocks and additional A circles to the design wall.

Quilt Assembly

1. Referring to the quilt assembly diagram, join 4 of the Four-Patch blocks for the upper left corner of the quilt. As you did before, center template B on the intersection of the 4 Four-Patch blocks. Trace template B and cut out the circle, saving the pieced circle for the border. Sew a floral A circle into the cutaway area.

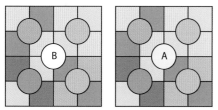

Make a 4-block unit and use template B to cut out a circle at the intersection. Then add circle A.

2. Join the first and second Four-Patch blocks of the bottom row.

3. Join the 2-block unit from Step 2 to the bottom of the 4-block unit from Step 1. Repeat the process of tracing template B, cutting out the circle over the center bottom intersection, and sewing in the A circle.

4. Join the 3 remaining Four-Patch blocks into a column on the right.

5. Join the 3-block column from Step 4 to the right side of the quilt body. Repeat the process of tracing template B, cutting out the circles in the 2 remaining intersections, and adding the floral A circles.

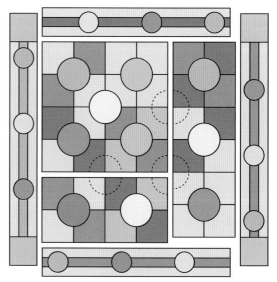

Quilt assembly. Dotted lines indicate final appliqué placement after quilt center is assembled.

Borders

1. Sew a floral 3½″ × 45½″ strip between 2 matching spotted floral 2½″ × 45½″ strips. Match the center and ends of the spotted floral border strips to the center floral strips and pin. Sew the strips together along the length. Press the seams toward the center strip.

2. Use pattern C to make a 5″ circle template from card stock. Refer to Preparing Appliqué Circles (page 22) to use the template with the four-patch circle that you cut from the block intersections. Place template C on the wrong side of the fabric. Pull the running stitch tight so that the fabric covers the circle and the running stitch is on the wrong side. Press the circle with a hot iron. Repeat to prepare 12 four-patch circles.

3. Position the pieced border sections around the quilt and arrange the four-patch circles in any placement you like. To mark your circle position, trace the template with a chalk pencil, mark the position with a pin, and then press a crease into the border strip. Pin, glue, or baste the circles in place, using the seams as guides for centering. Use your favorite method to appliqué the circles into place. Mark the top of each border strip to avoid confusion when joining the borders to the quilt body.

4. Matching the center and ends, pin and sew the top and bottom border sections to the quilt body.

5. Sew a floral 7½″ × 7½″ square to each end of the remaining border sections. Matching the center and ends, pin and sew the side borders to the quilt.

QUILTING

Ballroom Dancing was commercially quilted by Denise Biviano. She used an allover squiggle pattern that reminds me of the shoe pattern for dance-step instructions!

MIXING TEXTURES

There is a simplicity in drawing and cutting out shapes that awakens the child in us. The forgiving nature of the wool felt allows us to open up our imagination and make simple flowers, animals, and leaves with appliqué. The stitches can be simple or ornate, fancy or naïve. These two projects are easy and quick to make but will add long-lasting snapshots of happy color on the wall and the sofa! Let your imagination take control and release the inner child.

CHOOSING FABRICS

BACKGROUND   Big black polka dots on linen have just the right amount of mirth to support the silly figures. The vintage Japanese fabric is perfect for the tabletop covering. You can use anything that relates to the idea of a pot of toys on a table against a wallpaper backdrop.

INNER BORDER   The black-and-off-white stripe works to bring out the black lines and dots and to lead our eye into the border. Black-and-white fabrics always work with lots of color.

BORDER   These are the fabrics that make up my stash. I like the way they play together. The key is to bounce the cool colors off the warm colors, the small graphics against the big, and to balance the placement of the colors around the edge equally.

PARTY FAVORS

FINISHED QUILT: 40½″ × 52½″ (103 cm × 133 cm)

It is fun to let the imagination take over and just have a go with color and shapes in party mode. I love the idea of funky animals just hanging out among the flowers in this vase. The monkey, giraffe, and elephant just make me feel like turning the music up and dancing! Our house is full of a variety of textiles, so my Mexican-style vase is sitting on vintage Japanese fabric surrounded by color. Using wool felt allows for simple cutting of any shape you like. I started out with a black whipstitch to appliqué them all down and then realized I could do it on my machine with a triple straight stitch.

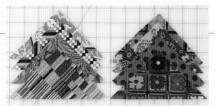

Gathering fabrics for the border is fun! Pick the most colorful combinations you can find with a variety of different-sized motifs. I make a pile of warm colors and a pile of cool colors. As I sew them together, I mix them up by alternating a selection from each group to create maximum impact. The inner border in black and white will always work with any palette.

WOOL Only the brightest will do! Select from good-quality wool that is color safe and washable. Hot pink, bright orange, lemon yellow—if it jumps off the background, it is good! The blacks and browns as well as the more muted colors only let the bright colors glow brighter.

BINDING Here I used a strong Kaffe Fassett stripe cut on the bias to wrap the colorful border around to the back.

MATERIALS

Yardage is based on 42"-wide (107 cm) fabric, unless otherwise stated.

- **Black-and-white dotted linen:** ⅝ yard (60 cm) for background

- **Colorful floral linen:** ½ yard (50 cm) for tablecloth

- **Animal and/or floral prints:** ¼ yard (25 cm) or a fat quarter of 2 different fabrics for stems (or 2 fabrics that remind you of stems)

- **Black-and-white stripe:** ½ yard (50 cm) for inner border

- **Assorted colorful prints:** 2 yards (2.3 m) total in scraps at least 10″ × 10″ (25 cm × 25 cm) and strips at least 5″ wide (15 cm) for outer border

- **Assorted colors of wool felt:** piece sizes ranging from 5″ × 5″ (15 cm × 15 cm) to 10″ × 10″ (25 cm × 25 cm)

- **Binding:** ½ yard (50 cm)

- **Backing:** 2⅞ yards (2.5 m)

- **Batting:** 49″ × 61″ (124 cm × 155 cm)

Notions:

- **Appliqué pins**

- **Perle cotton #8:** in black and assorted colors to your taste (I used a lot of red.)

- *Optional:* Half-square and quarter-square triangle rulers designed for cutting with strips

All measurements include the seam allowance. Refer to Favorite Techniques (page 17) for information about cutting strips and appliqué. Prepare templates from the Party Favors *patterns A–K (pullout page P3). Label the pieces as indicated.*

Black-and-white dotted linen:

- Cut a rectangle 20″ × 42″ for appliqué background.

Colorful floral Olinen:

- Cut a rectangle 20″ × 16″ for tablecloth background.

Animal and/or floral prints:

- Cut approximately 60″ of 1″-wide bias strips for the appliqué stems.

Wool felt:

- Use templates A–K to cut appliqué shapes from various colors.

Black-and-white stripe:

- Cut 2 strips 3½″ × 40½″ for inner side borders.
- Cut 2 strips 2½″ × 24½″ for inner top and bottom borders.

Assorted colorful prints:

- Cut 8 squares 9¼″ × 9¼″; subcut each diagonally twice to yield 4 quarter-square triangles (A) for a total of 32 A triangles for outer border.
- Cut 32 squares 4⅞″ × 4⅞″; subcut each diagonally once to yield 2 half-square triangles (B) for a total of 64 B triangles for outer border.

Binding fabric:

- Cut 6 strips 2½″ × width of fabric.

SEWING

All seam allowances are ¼″, unless otherwise noted.

Background Assembly

1. Place the dotted background 20″ × 42″ rectangle right side up on a cutting surface. Place the floral print 20″ × 16″ rectangle, also right side up, on top of the dotted rectangle, with the bottom and side edges aligned.

2. Using a rotary cutter and a straight-edge ruler, cut a diagonal line through both fabrics from about 4″ from the bottom left to about 14″ from the bottom right. Discard the fabric pieces that will not be part of the project.

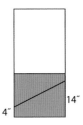

3. Flip the remaining floral fabric up over the remaining dotted background so that the right sides are together and the angled raw edges are aligned. Pin, stitch, and press to make the pieced background for the appliqué.

4. After appliquéing the quilt center, you will trim the background to 18½″ × 40½″, so mark the background with 18″ × 40″ boundaries and be sure to keep the appliqués inside the marks.

Appliqué

1. Make stems, using a ½″ bias tape maker to turn under the edges of the 1″ bias strip of animal print.

2. Refer to the quilt assembly diagram (next page) to place the stems and wool felt appliqué shapes on the background, being sure to keep within the 18″ × 40″ finished size of the background. Follow the arrangement in the quilt photo (next page) or use your own layout. Pin in place with appliqué pins.

3. Use decorative machine stitching or whipstitch the edges by hand, using black perle cotton #12.

tip

Check out the decorative machine stitches on your sewing machine as options for machine appliqué. I used a decorative triple straight stitch (stitch 713 on the BERNINA 750) to appliqué the pieces to the background. For machine appliqué, you may want to stabilize the background with a bit of wash-away stabilizer. See Resources (page 127).

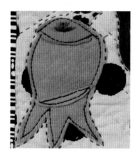

Inner Border

1. Trim the appliquéd background to 18½″ × 40½″.

2. Join the black-and-white 3½″ × 40½″ border strips to the sides of the background by matching the centers and ends. Pin and sew in place.

3. Join the black-and-white 2½″ × 24½″ border strips to the top and bottom of the background. Note that the top and bottom border strips are indeed more narrow than the side borders.

Outer Border

1. Mixing the warm and cool colors together, sew a B triangle to each short side of an A triangle to make a 4½″ × 8½″ Flying Geese block. Make a total of 32 blocks.

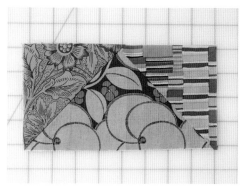

Pair warm and cool colors to make each Flying Geese block.

2. Make a pleasing arrangement of Flying Geese around the quilt center as shown in the quilt assembly diagram, noting the direction of the Flying Geese.

3. Join 2 rows of 3 Flying Geese for the top and bottom borders. Matching the centers and ends, sew the borders to the top and bottom of the quilt center.

4. Join 2 columns of 13 Flying Geese blocks for the side borders. To complete the quilt, match the centers and ends of the columns to the sides of the quilt. Sew the borders to the quilt.

Quilt assembly

QUILTING

The quilting is done with variegated perle cotton #12. When a project is an explosion of color, only the basic stabilizing quilt stitches are needed. Follow the lines of the quilt for guidance and keep it simple. Of course, if you prefer to go wild with your stitching, you could add more lines in the background, stipple on the machine, or choose any decorative pattern you like.

MAGPIE PILLOWS:
MAGPIE STROLLING AND MAGPIE IN FLIGHT

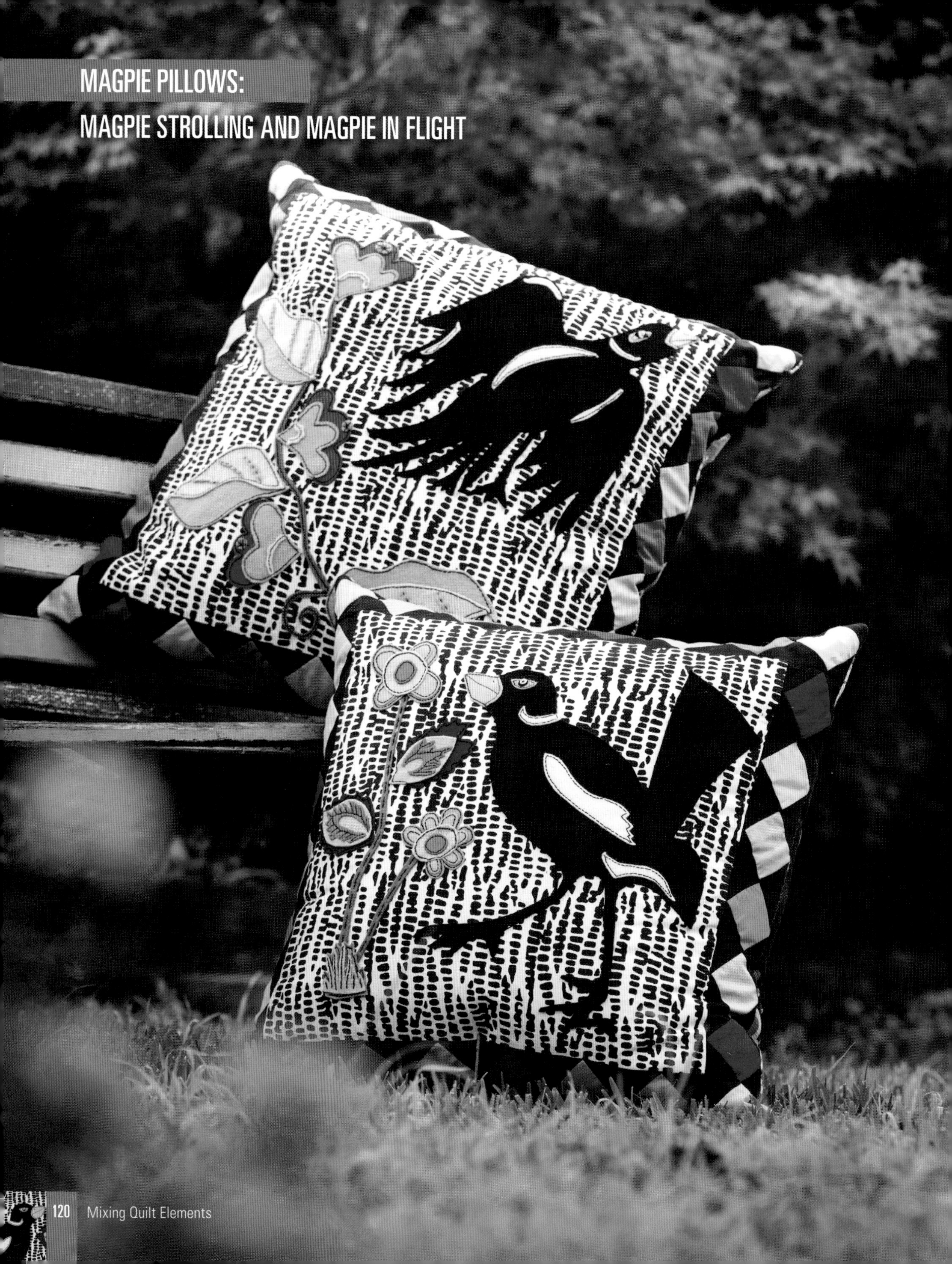

MAGPIE PILLOWS:
MAGPIE STROLLING
AND MAGPIE IN FLIGHT

FINISHED PILLOW: 24″ x 24″ (61 cm x 61 cm)

Many years ago I watched out the window as my father-in-law fed a magpie in the backyard. It became a memory of my father-in-law that lasted long after he had left us but also started my fascination with this crazy bird full of proud personality. Marching on the ground or in flight, they always seem to be in complete control.

I am a quilter, but in an attempt to try new things I decided to make a couple of pillows with invisible zippers. You can, if you choose, finish your pillows with any closure you prefer. In this case, I used the BERNINA invisible zipper foot and found it to be easy, quick, and a very nice finish.

CHOOSING FABRICS

BACKGROUND   This textural black-and-white print was designed by Reece Scannel. It has a great earthy feel to it that stands up to bright colors.

APPLIQUÉ   I used Italian wool felt for the appliqué. The flowers are bright and childlike in nature appliquéd with black perle cotton #12.

BORDERS   Black homespun / solid cotton is the perfect setting for rounds of colorful homespun squares. When I went to make the borders I decided to use the colors I had on hand rather than search for a perfectly matching combination. The slight variations and nonmatching effect is just what I was looking for as a border for the pillows.

MATERIALS

Yardage is based on 42"-wide (107 cm) fabric, unless otherwise stated.

- **Black-and-white textural print:** ⅝ yard (60 cm) for background for 2 pillows
- **Black homespun / solid cotton:** ½ yard (50 cm) for border triangles for 2 pillows
- **Backing:** ¾ yard (70 cm) for 2 pillows

Wool felt:

- **Black:** 2 rectangles 12" × 16" (30 cm × 41 cm)
- **Assorted colors:** piece sizes ranging from approximately 5" × 5" (15 cm × 15 cm) to 10" × 10" (25 cm × 25 cm)

Solid cottons:

- ⅛ yard (15 cm) each, in colors to coordinate with wool felt appliqué:

  For Magpie Strolling: orange, red, yellow, light blue, and light green

  For Magpie in Flight: yellow, aqua, red, pink, and lavender

Notions:

- **Zippers:** 2 invisible zippers, 20"
- **Pillow forms:** 2 inserts, 24" × 24" (61 cm × 61 cm)
- **Perle cotton #12:** in black

CUTTING

The cutting directions are for 2 pillows. Refer to Favorite Techniques (page 17) for information about cutting strips. Label the pieces as indicated.

Background:

- Cut 2 squares 19" × 19".

Black homespun / solid cotton:

- Cut 3 strips 4¼" × width of fabric; subcut 24 squares 4¼" × 4¼", and cut diagonally twice to yield 96 quarter-square triangles (C) for border setting triangles.
- Cut 1 strip 2⅜" × width of fabric; subcut 16 squares 2⅜" × 2⅜", and cut diagonally once to yield 32 half-square triangles (B) for border.

Solid cottons:

- Cut 6 or 7 squares 2⅝" × 2⅝" from each fabric for borders. You'll use only 56 squares (A).

Wool felt:

- See Appliqué Blocks (next page).

Backing:

- Cut 2 squares 24½" × 24½".

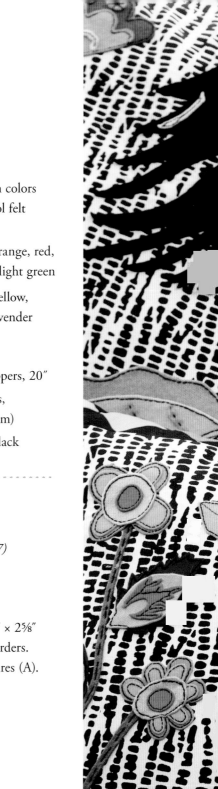

SEWING

All seam allowances are ¼".

Appliqué Blocks

Magpie in Flight appliqué pieces A–F

Magpie Strolling appliqué pieces G–N

1. The background 19″ × 19″ squares are oversized to allow for some shrinkage during appliqué. Mark the finished size (18″ × 18″) with a pencil before starting to avoid working outside the boundary.

2. Referring to Preparing Appliqué Shapes (page 22), make templates for the Magpie pillows, using patterns A–F for Magpie in Flight and patterns G–N for Magpie Strolling (pullout page P4). Trace the motifs onto freezer paper and cut out on the line. Lightly iron or pin the freezer paper to the wool. Trace around the freezer paper with a chalk pencil or felt-tip pen. Cut out the wool shapes. If you marked the wool with a pen, be sure to cut away the line.

3. Layer the designs from back to front. Appliqué the wool shapes on top to the shapes underneath, making each unit before you appliqué it to the background square. For example, appliqué the white details and eyes onto the birds before you appliqué the bird body to the background.

4. Fold the background in half both horizontally and vertically and press the seams. Work from the center out, pin, then backstitch or straight stitch the shapes onto the background.

5. After you have completed the appliqué, trim the background to 18½″ × 18½″.

note

Now, I know the temptation is strong to do exactly what you see, but feel free to cut the shapes out freehand and to place the motifs as you like!

Borders

1. Join a black B triangle to 2 adjacent sides of an A square. Press. Make 8 for each pillow. These will be the ends of the border rows.

Make 8 for each pillow.

2. Sew a C triangle to a unit from Step 1 as shown. Make 8 for each pillow. Set these aside.

Make 8 for each pillow.

3. Sew 2 C triangles to opposite sides of an A square as shown. Make 20 for each pillow.

Make 20 for each pillow.

4. For each pillow make 2 side border sections with 4 units from Step 3 between 2 units from Step 2.

Make 2 for each pillow.

5. For the top and bottom borders, make 2 border sections for each pillow with 6 units from Step 3 between 2 units from Step 2.

Make 2 for each pillow.

6. Refer to the quilt assembly diagram. For each pillow, sew the pieced border sections from Step 4 to the sides of the center. Then add the pieced border sections from Step 5 to the top and bottom.

Quilt assembly

QUILTING

You can quilt your pillow front if you desire, but I didn't quilt mine.

PILLOW ASSEMBLY WITH ZIPPER

An invisible zipper at the bottom side of the pillow provides a closure for these pillows.

1. Refer to the zipper manufacturer's instructions, but here's what I do: Open the zipper and work with one side of the zipper. With right sides together, pin the zipper to the pillow border, matching the center of the zipper with the pillow front center. Pin the zipper to the border through the points of the border squares, and pin the zipper ends to the border. Using an invisible zipper foot and starting at the open end of the zipper, stitch along the edge as far as possible.

2. With the zipper still open, pin the other side of the zipper to the pillow backing, matching the center of the zipper with the center of the backing and pinning the zipper ends to the backing. Start sewing at the open end of the zipper and sew along the edge as far as possible.

3. Take the pillow case out of the machine and close the zipper. Fold the front and back edges so that they meet, and finish sewing through both sides of the zipper. Sew along the end of the zipper to the end of the front and back.

4. With the zipper *open*, pin the pillow front to the back with right sides together. Sew around the remaining sides of the pillow, using a ¼″ seam allowance. I like to curve around the corners to eliminate some of the bulk.

5. Before turning the pillow case right sides out, fold the corners together. Fold the sides into the corner to capture the bulk of the seams with a pinch and hold them in place as you turn the pillow inside out. This helps to keep the corners full. Insert the pillow form.

Magpie Strolling

Magpie in Flight

ABOUT THE AUTHOR

Photo by John Doughty

Kathy Doughty is a self-taught quilter who has benefited from a vast array of experiences collected as a founding owner of Material Obsession in 2003.

Material Obsession is a patchwork shop in Sydney, Australia, that is known for innovation in contemporary designs and fabrics. It is a place where creative people go to stretch their fabric and technique comfort zones by thinking outside the square in all areas of quilt design. Working with customers, teachers, and industry leaders on a day-to-day basis for more than twelve years has given Kathy a unique skill base to which she attributes her eclectic style.

"When surrounded by supportive, generous, creative people, it is easy to feel that new direction is the norm," she says. Many of the concepts that define the current modern movement have been practiced at Material Obsession since its inception.

Having found quilting in her mid-30s, Kathy had to learn all there was to know about making a quilt from threading a machine to calculating seam allowance. She attributes her popular teaching methods to always remembering what it was like not to know anything.

"I never want to change the preferences of a quilter, but rather to create paths that expand what is already there," she says. Encouraging individual process and telling stories in quilts is critical to her quilting practice.

Mixing Quilt Elements is Kathy's fifth book. As well as designing quilts and writing patterns, she is now designing fabric. Her first two collections, A Wandering Mind and Trail Blazing, were produced for the Australian market. In 2015, Kathy joined the FreeSpirit Fabric design team and introduced Flock Together. The collections bring to life drawings from her imagination in a format designed to be used in quilts. Medallions, borders, sashing, backgrounds, and fussy-cutting elements are all considered.

The growth of the business has been very exciting. She now partners running the shop with her photographer husband, John, and a team of wonderfully creative women. As the shop has grown, she has collected a trusted group of talented designers to help keep fresh ideas on the menu every day. The women of Material Obsession are creative designers in their own right and bring a wealth of ideas to the design team.

Kathy has three grown sons in their early 20s. They are all keenly interested in creative endeavors of their own, from making art to music. She was born in the United States and worked in New York City for the duration of the 1980s before moving to California for a year, then to Sydney, Australia. She now calls Australia home but enjoys frequent trips to the United States to teach, go to Quilt Market, and visit family.

Her life is an open book on her blog, materialobsession.typepad.com. Follow her as @matobsgirl on Facebook or Instagram.

Also by Kathy Doughty:

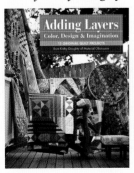 

The first place to go for information and products is your local quilt shop. If that is not possible or they cannot help you, then try the Internet for information.

Material Obsession   materialobsession.com.au
Fabrics, kits, and templates, including the Material Obsession 1″ Octagon and Square Set

C&T Publishing   ctpub.com
fast2cut HexEssentials Small (½″, ⅜″, ¾″, and 1″), 1½″, or 2½″ Viewers; Clearview Triangle 60° Acrylic Rulers; Wash-Away Stitch Stabilizer

Creative Grids   creativegridsusa.com
Rulers and templates

Karen Kay Buckley   karenkaybuckley.com
Perfect Circles and Bigger Perfect Circles

Jaybird Quilts   jaybirdquilts.com
Hex N More ruler by Julie Herman

Aurifil Threads   aurifil.com
40- and 50-weight all-cotton thread

Superior Threads   superiorthreads.com
Frosted Donut sets